RULING THE VOID

T0015600

RULING THE VOID

The Hollowing of Western Democracy

PETER MAIR

Editor's Foreword
by Francis Mulhern

Introduction to the Second Edition
by Chris Bickerton

VERSO
London • New York

Verso wishes to acknowledge the generous financial support of the
Department of Political and Social Sciences, European University Institute,
of which Peter Mair was a member at the time of his death.

This second edition published by Verso 2023
First published by Verso 2013, 2023
© Peter Mair 2013, 2023
Foreword © Francis Mulhern 2013, 2023
Introduction to the Second Edition © 2023

1 3 5 7 9 10 8 6 4 2

Verso
UK: 6 Meard Street, London W1F 0EG
US: 388 Atlantic Avenue, Brooklyn, NY 11217
versobooks.com

Verso is the imprint of New Left Books

ISBN-13: 978-1-83976-789-0
ISBN-13: 978-1-78168-234-0 (US EBK)
ISBN-13: 978-1-78168-540-2 (UK EBK)

British Library Cataloguing in Publication Data
A catalogue record for this book is available from the British Library

The Library of Congress Cataloged the Previous Edition as Follows:

Mair, Peter.
Ruling the void : the hollowing of Western democracy
    / Peter Mair.
pages cm
Includes bibliographical references and index.
ISBN 978-1-78168-099-5 (hardback : alk. paper) –
ISBN 978-1-84467-324-7 (pbk. : alk. paper)
    1. Democracy – Europe, Western. 2. Political
participation – Europe, Western. 3. Political parties –
Europe, Western. 4. Apathy – Europe, Western.
5. Skepticism – Europe, Western. I. Title.
JN94.A91M35 2013
320.94 – dc23
2013014147

Typeset in Sabon by MJ & N Gavan, Truro, Cornwall
Printed by CPI Group (UK) Ltd, Croydon CR0 4YY

For Tessa, John and Cathleen, 'brave new world ...'

CONTENTS

List of Tables	ix
Introduction to the Second Edition:	
Beyond the Void? by Chris Bickerton	xi
Editor's Foreword by Francis Mulhern	xxi
Introduction	1
Democracy and indifference	2
Indifference and renewal	8
Redefining democracy	13
1. The Passing of Popular Involvement	17
Citizen disengagement	20
Electoral participation	22
Electoral volatility	29
Party loyalties	35
Party membership	37
Conclusion	42
2. The Challenge to Party Government	45
Do parties matter?	52
Declining electoral cohesion	56

CONTENTS

The problem of party government   60
The waning of party government   65

3. The Withdrawal of the Elites   75
The century of mass politics   77
From civil society to the state: the location
    of parties   83
The functions of parties   89

4. Popular Democracy and the European
    Union Polity   99
Being safe for, or from, democracy   100
The EU polity   103
Politicization and displacement   109
Europeanization and depoliticization   115
The puzzle of apolitical Europe   119
The EU as a construct   125
Conclusion: Euroscepticism and
    polity-scepticism   137

Appendix: A Note on Additional Tables   143
Bibliography   149
Index   169

LIST OF TABLES

1. Record low levels of turnout in western
   Europe, 1950–2009   28
2. Record high levels of volatility in western
   Europe, 1950–2009   33
3. Trends in party identification in western
   Europe, 1960s–1990s   35
4. Party membership change in established
   democracies, 1980–2009   41
5. Vote share of populist parties in western
   Europe, general elections and European
   elections, 1979–2010   112

INTRODUCTION TO THE SECOND EDITION: BEYOND THE VOID?

Chris Bickerton

In his 2004 novel *Seeing*, Jose Saramago tells the story of a city cut off from the rest of the country. Encircled by government troops, it is the target of assassinations and a vicious media campaign. The government has abandoned the city to its fate, setting itself up in a new capital at a safe distance from the 'saboteurs' and 'terrorists'. What awful act by the city's inhabitants merited such a response? A vast majority of them – around 80 per cent – spoilt their ballot papers in a national election. Saramago is careful to point out that this was all the citizens did. There was no violence, no organized campaign against the government, no attempt to seize power. The mass uprising was uncoordinated and leaderless. Saramago's book is about the consequences of a massive withdrawal of consent by citizens in a democracy.

Those familiar with Peter Mair's classic study *Ruling the Void*, first published in 2013, will find many common threads with Saramago's novel. The Portuguese writer rendered as fiction what would become one of Mair's main insights, namely that democracy in the late

twentieth and early twenty-first century has experienced
a prolonged withdrawal by citizens from political life.
Just as Saramago's government sneaks out of the capital
in the dead of night, hoping that no one will notice them
leaving, Mair argues that the withdrawal of consent
is mirrored in the actions of the political class itself.
Though a far cry from the revolutionary acts of earlier
centuries, this withdrawal of consent is highly destabi-
lizing for democratic systems, much more dangerous in
fact than any stark opposition between rival ideologies
or political programmes. As Saramago's embattled politicians observe: 'All I need is to have the enemy in my
sights . . . But that is precisely the problem, we don't
know where the enemy is, we don't even know who they
are.'

Refined over the course of his academic career, and
summarized in remarkably clear prose in *Ruling the Void*,
Mair's arguments retain their originality and power.
Mair had analysed how party systems were traditionally
organized on an axis of regulated competition between
left and right. By the early 1990s, however, something
had begun to change. Slowly but surely, the familiar
ideological conflicts were losing their power, becoming – in the words of a former French prime minister
– *une langue morte*, a dead language. The scaffolding of
socialism versus Christian democracy might still supply
the outward façade of national political systems, but
party politics had been recast around a new dynamic.
Jettisoning their ideological programmes, parties now
resembled one another more and more. For Mair, this
convergence was not just a product of global pressures
such as the rise of neoliberalism, or the increasing power
of international regimes and regional organizations like
the European Union. It was also a product of changes
within the parties themselves. Cut off from voters, they
survived through their links to the state apparatus.

'Left versus Right' had given way to 'Us versus Them', as people increasingly considered politicians to be a standalone political class, a *casta*, identifiable by media soundbites and identikit television appearances.

Politicians were viewed with a mixture of scepticism, fatalism and disdain. Similar sentiments prevailed amongst the governing classes: voters appeared to them as an unruly and truculent mass, manageable only through focus groups and occasional visits to town centres and housing estates, where interaction between governors and the governed was kept to a minimum. Followers of British politics will not have forgotten Prime Minister Gordon Brown's disastrous walkabout in Rochdale in 2010, when he was caught on camera describing a voter as a 'bigoted woman'. Labour's election campaign never recovered.

A void had thus opened up between society and politics: the mass of citizens on one side, politicians on the other. Tellingly, the best political dramas of the period – from *West Wing* to *Borgen* – focused their attention on the internal workings of the political bubble, with virtually none of the action taking place outside government offices and television studios.

Some observers of politics have continued to use the old map of left–right politics to navigate their way around these new realities. Others have declared that democracy itself is on its deathbed. Mair pursued a different path. He explored how the void was reshaping political life, creating new sorts of slimmed-down political parties and new types of politicians. It also generated a different style of politics, crude and expletive-filled, as captured in Armando Iannucci's *The Thick of It* and *Veep* – uncontained vitriol accompanied by a striking lack of substance.

The institutional transformation of political parties has been far-reaching. Historically, modern political parties were a product of two trends. One was the decision of the organized labour movement – after much uncertainty and internal deliberation – to embrace nascent forms of parliamentarism. This saw the creation of political organizations tasked with representing the interests of labour in an age of representative government, from the German Social Democratic Party (est. 1863) and the Swedish Social Democratic Party (1889) to the British Labour Party (1900). The other trend was the response by existing parliamentary groups to the expansion of the franchise. Aware that the advent of mass politics was presenting them with challenges but also many opportunities, conservative factions within legislatures began to organize themselves at local level. This gave birth to what we now think of as the classical model of the party, with its different organizational strata: on the ground, in central office and in parliament. It was an institution that translated social conflicts – struggles between labour and capital, confessional religious conflicts, tensions between town and country – into a political programme for government. The party thus incarnated the fusion between society and politics characteristic of twentieth-century mass politics.

Parties in the age of Peter Mair's void are a very different beast. Simple platforms for office-seeking leaders, they have steadily pushed aside party activists and officials. Newcomers to the political scene cultivate direct ties with voters in an effort to circumvent the clunky intermediary layers of the traditional party. When Silvio Berlusconi set up his own political movement, *Forza Italia!*, in 1994, he went out of his way to avoid holding any of his party meetings in old Democrazia Cristiana buildings. Instead of synthesizing societal divisions into an identifiable programme via the deliberative mechanisms of a national party conference or congress, political parties today hire outside experts and polling consultants to tell them what 'the people' think and what issues they should campaign on. In 2007, Sarkozy tasked Boston Consultants with the drafting of his centre-right party's election manifesto. He also paid for the same consultants to teach his Gaullist deputies how to sell their message to the public. In 2017, Emmanuel Macron's political offer – to do away with the established political class and to orient the system toward pragmatic problem-solving – originated in an extensive on-the-ground polling exercise, undertaken by a small group working under his personal guidance. He called his new party En Marche! so the name would coincide with his own initials.

The opening of the void has meant that parties have to be creative in their ways of financing themselves, membership dues giving way to reliance on private donations. In some countries, state funding has provided a lifeline, but it has not removed murkier sources of party finance. The decades which Mair associates with the decline and eventual crisis of 'party democracy' coincide with an almost never-ending litany of corruption scandals – from the illicit financing of the German Christian Democratic Union (CDU), which badly damaged the reputation of Helmut Kohl, to the short-lived political career of Austria's one-time political golden boy, ex-chancellor Sebastien Kurz. As part of his reinvention of the centre-right People's Party (ÖVP), Kurz was accused of using public money to support the publication of opinion polls favourable to the ÖVP and likely to help its election prospects.

'My generation, it's all, you know, apaffy, that's what it's like . . . Apaffy.' These are the words of Duffy, the unconventional private detective created by Julian Barnes writing under the pseudonym Dan Kavanagh. The Duffy series spanned the 1980s and Barnes was describing the effects of Margaret Thatcher's political assault on the organized labour movement in Britain. Mair's book traces the rise of political apathy: the decline in turnout at elections, the rise in electoral volatility as voters no longer feel any loyalty towards a particular party, and the fall in numbers of card-carrying party members.

Ruling the Void was written before the mass protests in the Puerta del Sol in Madrid in 2011, and before the Brexit referendum of June 2016 and the dramatic parliamentary aftermath. It predates the election of Donald Trump, #MeToo and Black Lives Matter, and the fleeting Corbynization of the British Labour Party. Whereas Mair documented an era of increasing depoliticization, since the book's publication (and Mair's untimely death) we have seen new forms of political radicalism emerge, from Bernie Sanders and Alexandria Ocasio-Cortez in the United States to the apotheosis of far-right identitarian nationalism in the rhetoric of France's Eric Zemmour.

Mair's book documented politics in a largely analogue era. The 1990s, however remarkable it may seem to us now, was a decade almost without mobile phones. The now familiar association of all political ills with the rise of social media came at the very end of the period Mair was documenting: Twitter was founded in 2006 and Apple launched its first iPhone at the beginning of 2007. Has the era captured in *Ruling the Void* now passed? Was Mair's book primarily an analysis of that 'generation without a name', as the French documentarist Ovidie put it – the generation caught between the transformative power of the baby boomers and the radical stridency of generation Z? Mair opened his *Ruling the Void* with the much-quoted phrase 'the age of party democracy is over'. Perhaps it is the crisis of party democracy that is now over.

Evidence suggests that our politics have become more divisive and fractious – from the high numbers of

Republican voters who question the legitimacy of the US presidential election of 2020 to the emergence of far-right populist parties in countries hitherto insulated from this sort of politics, such as Spain and Estonia. But what do we really mean by political polarization? In some places, deep-seated ideological polarization has indeed begun to reshape society and politics. Chile's experiment in constitutional revision is a case in point. After a massive and sustained social revolt in 2019, a convention was given the task of drafting a new constitutional settlement. In an attempt to lock in social democratic politics, public healthcare and education, a nationalized mining industry and many other reforms were included but the new constitution was overwhelmingly rejected in a referendum in the early autumn of 2022. Thirty years after the country's transition to democracy, political enfranchisement is slowly translating into significant social change but at the cost of immense polarization and conflict.

In Western Europe, Mair's principal focus, something rather different has occurred. The continued convergence between parties – evident in the German SPD's successful bid to carry Merkel's policies into a post-Merkel era – coexists alongside a hostile and vicious form of political debate. It is a paradox that as political discourse has become more and more ill-tempered, the issues around which politicians disagree narrows.

A decade on from the publication of *Ruling the Void*, we have seen changes in levels of participation and political mobilization. But the contentious, citizen-driven politics of the 2010s, from the Indignados in Spain to the piazzas across Italy full to the brim with supporters of Beppe Grillo's Movimento Cinque Stelle, were *expressions* of the void that Peter Mair documented more than they were evidence of the void being overcome. They were directed against collusion between the mainstream parties – in Spain, the centre-right Partido Popular (PP) and the centre-left Socialist Party (PSOE) were dismissed as one unitary block, the 'PPSOE' – and against the venality of the political class itself. Products of the post-2008 economic crisis and articulating a long-standing sense of political disenfranchisement, these movements were exactly what one might expect when apathy turns to anger, but under conditions of a stark separation between politics and society.

A more complex phenomenon has been the return of traditional ideologies to political parties that had tried to consign these ideas to history. The British Labour Party in the years after Jeremy Corbyn's successful bid to become leader in 2015 is one of the most interesting cases. The hollowed-out 'New' Labour Party had been a key inspiration for Peter Mair's writings; the return of ideological radicalism to the party should imply a move beyond the politics of the void. A closer analysis suggests otherwise. Certainly, Corbyn was able to halt and reverse the secular trend downwards in party membership: from around 200,000 members in 2014, the number of members had swelled to around 600,000 two years later, a development widely referred to as 'the Corbyn factor'. As well as boosting membership numbers, Corbynism injected ideological zeal back into the deflated carcass of the post-Blair party. For a time, the success of this endeavour seemed in the balance: the Corbyn-led Labour Party was able to strip Theresa May of her majority at her ill-judged 2017 general election. Two years later, in the 2019 'Brexit election', hopes were high. Some figures involved in the Sanders movement in the United States crossed the Atlantic, hoping to witness 'the British road to socialism'.

In the event, Corybn lost heavily. The Conservatives, led by Boris Johnson, secured a landslide majority, winning seats that had never before elected anything other than a Labour Party member of parliament. The lesson here is that Peter Mair's void cannot simply be overcome by capturing an existing party and transforming its programme and positions. Corbynism was the revival of ideological politics in a social vacuum. The core support for the Labour Party in 2017 and again in 2019 was in London and other urban centres across the UK – in the Midlands and in Greater Manchester and Merseyside. Elsewhere, its voters clustered in prosperous university towns and progressive coastal strongholds such as Brighton. Beyond this social bubble, Corbynism had little purchase.

Ruling the Void is a story of politics and society coming apart. A reversal of this trend cannot come from changes taking place within parties and the political sphere alone; nor can the void be filled in by changes in society that do not touch upon our politics. As citizens and politicians continue to confront one another in a relationship marked by a curious mixture of antagonism and indifference, Mair's book is more relevant than ever.

EDITOR'S FOREWORD

Francis Mulhern

Ruling the Void is the sombre title Peter Mair chose for the book he set out to write late in 2007, at Verso's suggestion. His sub-title summarized his concern in the plainest terms: it was 'the hollowing of Western democracy'. Mair's intention was to develop the arguments he had advanced in an article in *New Left Review*, marshalling the evidence of declining popular political participation across the longer-established democracies of Europe and tracking the same processes of withdrawal and disengagement in Europe as a whole and in the wider world. 'This hollowing of democracy has become a very widespread process', he wrote in his treatment for the book, 'particularly noticeable since the end of the Cold War.' It 'characterizes most of the advanced democracies, and is already evident in many of the new post-communist democracies. Across contemporary Europe, it is both symptomized and facilitated by the growing competences accorded to the deliberately depoliticized institutions of the EU. But it is also visible outside Europe, and particularly in North America.' At the heart of Mair's analysis was the concept of the political party as a vehicle of social interests, as an organizer of citizens and also of governance, in its successive forms from the mass parties of the first phase of general suffrage to the 'cartel parties' of recent times. His central judgement was decided and grave: 'the age of party democracy has passed', he wrote, in the opening sentence of his introduction, and with that a whole phase in the history of what we have known as democratic government.

This was a very large claim, even from an author well known among his disciplinary colleagues in political science for his willingness to pose large, difficult questions, to which he brought richly informing and subtilizing personal experience. Peter Mair was born on 3 March 1951 and grew up in the village of Rosses Point on the north-western coast of Ireland, the youngest child of Scots and Irish parents of differing religious dispositions, in years when the presumptions of the official nation and the Catholic Church went largely unchecked in the Irish Republic, and a precocious socialist in a political climate where red scares were respectable and potent. After school he entered University College Dublin (where we met, on the eve of our first classes). His initial studies were in history, economics and mathematics – along with English literature, for a time, just for pleasure. But politics claimed him once and for all, and after graduating in History and Politics he turned to the specialism he went on to practise with such distinction. There followed lectureships in the universities of Limerick and Strathclyde, the European University Institute (Florence) and Manchester. Peter was awarded his doctorate at Leiden – for a study that soon became a standard work, *The Changing Irish Party System* (1987) – and moved to teach there in 1990, the year in which he published his prize-winning study (co-written with Stefano Bartolini), *Identity, Competition and Electoral Availability*. Two years later came *Representative Government in Modern Europe* (with Michael Gallagher and Michael Laver) and his appointment as Professor of Political Science and Comparative Politics. His last move was to the European University Institute, which he had first joined as a research assistant and doctoral student in 1978 and to which he now returned, twenty-seven years later, as an internationally recognized master in his special field of political parties and party systems, to take up the chair in Comparative Politics. This record of institutional affiliations is first of all the index of an impressively hard-working and fruitful academic career, to be set beside the many other marks of achievement and esteem in a crowded curriculum vitae – editorships, senior disciplinary responsibilities, visiting appointments, inaugural and commemorative lectures – and, not least, the abundant, unprompted personal testimony of colleagues and students. Beyond that, however, it also traces an individual history of migration. Not just travel, which any reasonably successful academic can expect, in the form of trips to conferences and guest lectures (and there were many of them too), but migration as an experience of resettlement, in this case repeated and plural, of personal reorientation in new cultural and social conditions. Peter's parents had travelled long distances, in the special circumstances of imperial and wartime service: his Scots father served in the Indian Army, and met his future wife, a military nurse, in North Africa, eventually settling with her in Ireland. Their son travelled easily and settled more readily than most people ever do, making his career abroad from the age of twenty-five, living for significant periods in a total of five European countries. After Ireland, Scotland: Peter was proud of his mixed antecedents, and the Scots word *outwith*, which he came upon in Glasgow and quickly came to cherish as both indispensable and untranslatable, stayed with him, like a keepsake, through all his subsequent migrations. His time in the Netherlands was the longest of his adult life – fifteen years, after his first spell in Italy and a further six years in England – and personally the most significant to him: it was there that he married and had children. Italy, where the family moved in 2005, was already a home of another kind, along with Ireland the country of his longest working association, where from earliest days visiting friends were struck to re-encounter this man so completely familiar from past settings yet so calmly absorbed in his new one. Calm and curiosity together were the defining qualities of Peter's intellectual disposition, indeed, and his gift to the many who benefited from his teaching and writing. Something akin to the comparativism he upheld as a precept of rational inquiry was already present as ethos, in his way of being.

Throughout, for Peter, Ireland remained fundamental. He returned frequently for family holidays. Irish writing featured prominently in his eclectic personal canon: alongside Chandler, Vonnegut and Lodge sat Heaney and Flann O'Brien, and others particularly associated with his home region, Yeats, most eminently, and John McGahern. The country itself was a continuing special academic interest, and he maintained active working relations with the department in which he had studied in UCD. Of course, the engagement with Irish politics had always been more than academic. Peter was active in the controversies that divided the student left in the early seventies, most notably those over the crisis in the North at the defining moment of Bloody Sunday, and the prospect of Ireland's entry into the European Economic Community. He was also an active journalist at that time, and writing for newspapers and non-specialist magazines (print and latterly also online) continued to be a part of his intellectual repertoire, in Ireland, where he wrote for the *Irish Times* and *Magill*, and also in the other countries he lived in: the UK (*New Left Review, London Review of Books, Independent*), Netherlands (*Beleid en Maatschappij*) and Italy (*Reset*). The emerging emphasis of his interventions was the need for popular-democratic reforms in the countries of the European Union – most notably perhaps in Ireland, where he spoke on public platforms and acted as adviser to the pressure group We the Citizens, calling for reform of the Irish political system – and in the central political institutions of the EU itself. *Ruling the Void* was to synthesize years of scientific and scholarly work in that critical perspective.

For several years, work on the book went steadily forward, whether in the direct form of draft chapters filling out an evolving compositional scheme or, indirectly, in scholarly papers of substantial overlapping interest – but was then foreclosed on 15 August 2011, when Peter Mair died suddenly, on holiday in Ireland, aged just sixty. The volume now presented here brings together both kinds of writing, from the last six years of his life, in an effort to create a coherent, although necessarily incomplete, version of the book he set out to write, conveying something of the moral temper as well as the scientific and scholarly gifts he brought to his thinking about the prospects for democracy today. The work will speak for itself; the point of this foreword is simply to explain to readers how those writings have been made into this book.

Of the four texts that were available for the purpose, the first and longest is the partial manuscript of the Verso book. This is a continuous piece of writing seventy-seven pages long and marked 'working draft'. It appears here in the form in which it was left, as the introduction and chapters 1, 2 and 3 of *Ruling the Void*, with some editorial modification: the text has been copy-edited throughout in the ordinary way, and some lines elucidating the notion of 'the cartel party' have been borrowed from draft material for another book-length work in progress, *Democracy and the Cartelization of Political Parties*, this one co-authored with Richard S. Katz.

The other three texts are in one sense or another published works: 'Popular democracy and the European Union polity', European Governance Papers C-05-03, May 2005; 'Political opposition and the European Union', *Government and Opposition*, 42:1, 2007; 'Smaghi *vs*. the parties: representative government and institutional constraints', Conference on Democracy in Straitjackets: Politics in an Age of Permanent Austerity, Ringberg Castle, Munich, March 2011. The first of these very amply makes good one of the most important missing elements in the fragmentary draft: a discussion of the political institutions of the European Union, as distinct from the European nation-states whose polities are the main focus of the first three chapters. The remaining two papers are for different reasons not suitable for inclusion in their entirety: one substantially reiterates the content of the 2005 paper, and the other rests on a detailed, time-limited case study not in keeping with the generalizing manner of the draft. However, it was clear that both could help to make good a second regrettable lack – the absence of a full discussion of the general significance of populist oppositions in today's advanced democracies, a matter which, although certainly one of the preoccupations of 'Popular Democracy', was to have had a chapter to itself in the scheme of *Ruling the Void*. With this in view, I have transposed relevant passages from these papers into the main text on the EU polity, which, with ordinary copy-editing and some structural adjustment, now makes a long Chapter 4. Full details appear in the notes at the relevant places.

Thus, the book as it now appears corresponds in content to five of the seven chapters originally proposed, and includes one unforeseen at the outset, devoted to the crisis of party as a governmental form. While chapters on advanced democracies outside Europe, most notably the United States, and on the historical prospect of a 'partyless democracy' are lost to us, there are numerous indications, general and sometimes direct, of what Peter Mair might have said about the former and a great deal to suggest how he viewed the latter. *Ruling the Void* as we have it is about Europe, chiefly the older democracies of its western zone, and the transnational polity of the European Union, but the vision it offers is quite general, as if renewing in its own idiom the classic warning, *de te fabula narratur* – this story is about you.

Two further editorial measures call for particular mention. The first was the decision to supplement the prose of Chapter 4 with a pair of tables setting out the electoral record of the west European populist oppositions over the past thirty-odd years. The intention here – again – was to help offset the absence of a full discussion of this political phenomenon, while taking care not to introduce any new element of evaluation into the existing prose. The second was technical, and concerns the scholarly apparatus. The fragmentary draft, although referenced throughout, was left without its supporting bibliography – understandably – and the complete, integrated bibliography included here has been built up beginning from those included in the three already-published texts. These two specialized tasks have been carried out by Camille Bedock, a researcher in the European University Institute, to whom I offer my warm thanks.

I have also to thank Dick Katz, who very kindly made available the draft material from *Democracy and the Cartelization of Political Parties*, which he continues to work on. Above all, I am grateful to Karin Tilmans, Peter's wife, for her help and encouragement.

INTRODUCTION

The age of party democracy has passed. Although the parties themselves remain, they have become so disconnected from the wider society, and pursue a form of competition that is so lacking in meaning, that they no longer seem capable of sustaining democracy in its present form. *Ruling the Void* is about this problem. It deals with the problem of parties, of governments and of political representation in contemporary European democracy, and stems from a wider concern with the fracturing politics of popular democracy. It deals with how the changing character of political parties impacts upon their standing, legitimacy, and effectiveness, and thereby also on the standing, legitimacy and effectiveness of modern democracy. Although focused on Europe, and highlighting problems that are of particular relevance to Europe, the implications of the argument run much more widely.

The position that is developed here owes much to E.E. Schattschneider's *The Semi-Sovereign People* (1960) and to his contention that control over political decision-making sometimes lay beyond the reach of the ordinary citizen. This was a familiar theme in the political science of the 1960s, and was echoed in different ways, and differently contested, by a variety of critical scholars in the so-called pluralist-elitist debate. But although that particular debate has since been put to rest, Schattschneider's thesis continues to be highly relevant – although now in a stronger and less hesitant form. Indeed, almost a half-century later, it seems that even semi-sovereignty is slipping away, and that the people, or the ordinary citizenry, are becoming effectively *non*-sovereign. What we now see emerging is a notion of democracy that is being steadily stripped of its popular component – easing away from the demos.

As I try to show in this book, much of this has to do with the failings of contemporary political parties. I am not suggesting that there has been wholesale failure here. Rather, I am seeking to draw attention to an ongoing process in which there are party failings, in which democracy tends to adapt to these failings, and in which there is then a self-generating momentum whereby the parties become steadily weaker and democracy becomes even more stripped down.

DEMOCRACY AND INDIFFERENCE

When I first began to consider the notion of non-sovereignty, I associated it primarily with indifference: indifference towards politics, on the one hand, and indifference towards democracy, on the other. Indifference has always been one of the more neglected elements in the study of the relationship between citizens and politics, and its importance seemed to be badly underestimated by much of the literature on political trust and mistrust that emerged in the late 1990s. From my reading, the real problem at issue here was not trust as such, at least in the sense of there being a problem of popular mistrust of politicians and governments; rather, it was one of interest, or lack of interest, such that the sense of hostility that some citizens clearly felt towards the political class seemed less important than the indifference with which many more citizens viewed the political world more generally. To put it another way, whether politicians were liked or disliked, trusted or distrusted, seemed to matter less than whether they were seen as having a real bearing on citizens' life situations. Of course, the dividing line between indifference and hostility is not always very pronounced, and, as Alexis de Tocqueville once observed in the case of the old French aristocracy, it is easy to breed contempt for those who continue to claim privileges on the basis of functions they no longer fulfil. But even if indifference does lead on to hostility or lack of trust, it remains an important phenomenon in its own right, and hence it is also important to recognize that politics and politicians might simply be deemed irrelevant by many ordinary citizens (see also van Deth, 2000).

Indifference to politics and politicians was not just a problem on the ground, and was not simply confined to what could be seen in the realm of popular culture and attitudes. It was also compounded by the new rhetoric being employed by various politicians in the late 1990s, as well as by a growing anti-political sentiment that could be seen in the specialist literature on policy-making, institutional reform, and governance. Here too it seemed that politics as a process was often being denigrated or devalued, and that indifference to politics was deepening still further. Within the world of the politicians, the most obvious case was that of Tony Blair, who famously set himself up as being a leader above politics and political partisanship. 'I was never really in politics,' he claimed in a BBC2 television interview broadcast on 30 January 2000, during his first term as prime minister. 'I never grew up as a politician. I don't feel myself a politician even now.' Blair was also at pains to caution against the belief that politics could solve problems. For him, the purpose of the new 'progressive' agenda was not to provide solutions from above, but to help citizens to search for their own solutions – 'to help people make the most of themselves'. Politics in this sense was not about exercising the 'directive hand' of government, but about the synergy that could be generated by combining 'dynamic markets' with 'strong communities'. (Blair, 2001). In an ideal world, it seemed, politics would rapidly become redundant. As one of his close cabinet colleagues, Lord Falconer, was later to remark, 'depoliticizing of key decision-making is a vital element in bringing power closer to the people' (Flinders and Buller, 2004).

At one level, this was a simple populist strategy – employing the rhetoric of 'the people' as a means of underlining the radical break with past styles of government. At another level, however, it was an approach that gelled perfectly well with the tenets of what were then seen as newly emerging schools of governance – and with the idea that 'society is now sufficiently well organized through self-organizing networks that any attempts on the part of government to intervene will be ineffective and perhaps counterproductive' (Peters, 2002: 4). In this perspective, government becomes subordinate and deferential, and no longer seeks to wield power or even exercise authority. The relevance of government declines while that of non-governmental institutions and practices increases. In Ulrich Beck's terms, the dynamic migrates from politics with a capital P to politics with a small p – or to what he sometimes calls 'sub-politics' (e.g., Beck, 1992: 183–236). ·

Anti-political sentiments were also becoming more evident in the more specialized policy-making literature of the late 1990s. In 1997, Alan S. Blinder published an influential article in *Foreign Affairs* expressing his concern that government in the United States was becoming 'too political' (Blinder, 1997). Blinder, who was then a leading professor of economics and deputy head of the Federal Reserve, and hence a weighty contributor to this debate, suggested extending the model of the Federal Reserve in particular, and that of independent central banks in general, to other key policy areas, in such a way that decisions on health policy, welfare provision and so on would be taken out of the hands of elected politicians and passed over to the control of objective non-partisan experts. According to Blinder, the solutions that politics could offer were often sub-optimal, and hence the role of politicians in policy-making should be marginalized, or at least confined to those difficult areas in which the judgement of experts would not be sufficient to legitimize outcomes.

Similar arguments were then emerging in the European context. In 1996, for example, Giandomenico Majone argued that the role of expert decision-making in the policy-making process was superior to that of political decision-making in that the former could better take account of long-term interests. Politicians, by definition, worked only in the short-term, or at least were only capable of committing themselves in the short term, and hence to cede control of policy-making to politicians, allowing decisions to be dominated by considerations of the electoral cycle, was to risk less than optimal outcomes: 'the segmentation of the democratic process into relatively short time periods has serious negative consequences when the problems faced by society require long-term solutions'. The solution, echoing Blinder's advocacy of the Federal Reserve model, was to delegate powers to institutions 'which, by design, are not directly accountable to voters or to their elected representatives' (Majore, 1996: 10, 3). Majone described these institutions as 'non-majoritarian',[1] with more than one beneficial effect in decision-making. In particular, experts had many advantages over politicians when it came to dealing with the complexities of modern law-making, and with the many technical problems that often stymied or confused elected politicians. As traditional forms of state control were replaced by more complex regulatory frameworks, expertise rather than political judgement was likely to prove more valuable and effective (Majone, 2003: 299). Here too, then, politics was becoming devalued, with the potential contribution of politicians themselves to the policy process being seen as irrelevant or even damaging.

By the late 1990s, in short, it seemed that neither the citizens, on the one hand, nor the policy-makers, on the other, were keen to privilege the role of political or partisan decision-making. Even the new breed of third-way politician seemed ready to take a back seat. As far as politics was concerned, and perhaps even as far as the democratic process more generally was concerned, expert reason was deemed superior to interest. But while the various sources of evidence did indeed point to widespread indifference to politics and politicians,

---

1. There is some sleight-of-hand in this definition. Majone (1996: 12) comes to the notion of non-majoritarian institutions via a reference to Lijphart's (1984) distinction between majoritarian and consensus democracies, and hence, by implication, his idea of non-majoritarianism is equivalent to Lijphart's idea of consensus. This is not in fact the case, however. In contrast to Lijphart's idea of consensus democracy, which depends on elections, parties and political accountability, Majone's non-majoritarian institutions are depoliticized and expressly removed from the electoral and partisan process. For Lijphart, the contrast with majoritarian democracy is consensus democracy; for Majone, it is expert rule, or non-democracy.

they seemed to offer a much less robust foundation for the notion of indifference towards democracy as such. Indeed, the extensive debates about constitutional reform at that time, in public forums as well as in the more theoretical literature, gave the impression of a burgeoning interest in democracy, with more attention being paid to how democratic systems worked and to what they meant in reality, than probably at any stage in the previous twenty or thirty years. Democracy was on the agenda in the late 1990s, and, far from being treated with indifference, had become a research priority within both empirical political science and political theory. Already in 1997, for example, David Collier and Steven Levitsky were able to document some 500 different scholarly uses of the term, a number that has probably increased even more substantially since then, while the catalogues of academic publishers were beginning to brim over with new titles on the subject. Democracy was also becoming more of an issue on the everyday political agenda, with debates on institutional reform taking on a substantial role in a large number of western polities, appeals to 'participatory governance' issuing from the World Bank and other international organizations, and discussions of the reform of the European Union polity achieving a degree of salience that would have been almost unimaginable ten years before – as, for example, could be seen in the discussion of the European Commission White Paper on Governance in 2001, with its attention to participation and openness. By the end of the 1990s, democracy – whether associative, deliberative, or reflective; global, transnational, or inclusive; electoral, illiberal, or even just Christian – was at the centre of animated debate. At these levels at least – that is, institutionally and within the academy – indifference did not seem to figure.

INDIFFERENCE AND RENEWAL

Which leads me to my first puzzle. This massive renewal of interest in democracy coexists with indications of an opposite kind. In the political discourse of the twenty-first century we can see clear and quite consistent evidence of popular indifference to conventional politics, and we can also see clear evidence of an unwillingness to take part in the sort of conventional politics that is usually seen as necessary to sustain democracy. How do we square these developments?

There are two possibilities. The first is that they are in fact related, and that the growing intellectual and institutional interest in democracy is in part a response to the expansion of popular indifference. In other words, we get a lot of discussion about democracy, its meanings, and its renewal, at the moment when ordinary citizens begin to pull away from conventional forms of democratic engagement. Making democracy relevant comes on to the agenda at the time when it otherwise risks becoming irrelevant. However, while the timing suggests that this may be the case, the actual content of the discussion suggests a different story, and this leads to the second possibility. For, far from seeking to encourage greater citizen participation, or trying to make democracy more meaningful for the ordinary citizen, many of the discussions of institutional reforms, on the one hand, and of the theory of democracy, on the other, seem to concur in favouring options that actually discourage mass engagement. This can be seen, for example, in the emphasis on stakeholder involvement rather than electoral participation that is to be found in discussions of both associative democracy and participatory governance, as well as in the emphasis on the sort of exclusive and reasoned debate that is a hallmark of deliberative and reflective models of democracy. In neither case is much real scope afforded to conventional modalities of mass democracy. It can also be seen in the new emphasis that is placed on output-oriented legitimacy – with criteria such as efficiency, stability or continuity – in discussions of the European Union polity, and in the related idea that democracy in the EU requires 'solutions that are "beyond the state" and, perhaps, also beyond the conventions of western-style representative liberal democracy' (Shaw, 2000: 291). In other words, while there may be some concern with the problem of popular indifference to democracy, the idea of making democracy more mass-user friendly does not seem to be a frequently favoured answer. For Philip Pettit (2001: §46), for example, who discusses the issue of democratic renewal in the context of deliberation and depoliticization, the issue comes on to the agenda because 'democracy is too important to be left to the politicians, or even to the people voting in referendums.' For Fareed Zakaria (2003: 248), in his more popular account, renewal is necessary because 'what we need in politics today is not more democracy but less'.

Hence the second possibility: the renewal of interest in democracy and its meanings at the intellectual and institutional levels is not intended to open up or reinvigorate democracy as such; the aim is rather to redefine democracy in such a way that it can more easily cope with, and adapt to, the decline of popular interest and engagement. Far from being an answer to disengagement, the contemporary concern with renewing democracy is about coming to terms with it. In other words, what we see here is a wide-ranging attempt to define democracy in a way that does not require any substantial emphasis on popular sovereignty – at the extreme, the projection of a kind of democracy without the demos at its centre.

Part of this process of redefinition involves highlighting the distinction between what has been called 'constitutional democracy', on the one hand, and 'popular democracy', on the other, a distinction that overlaps with and echoes Robert Dahl's (1956) earlier contrast between 'Madisonian' and 'populistic' forms of democracy.[2] On the one hand, there is democracy's constitutional component – the component that emphasizes the need for checks and balances across institutions and entails government *for* the people. On the other hand, there is the popular component – which emphasizes the role of the ordinary citizen and popular participation, and which entails government *by* the people. These two distinct functions coexist and complement one another. However, though conceived of as two elements within a 'unified' sense of democracy, they are now becoming disaggregated, and then being contrasted with one another both in theory and practice. Hence, for example, the notions of 'illiberal' or 'electoral' democracy (Diamond, 1996; Zakaria, 1997) that have emerged since the collapse of the European communist bloc in 1989, and the attempt to understand those new 'democracies' that combined free elections – popular democracy – with restrictions on rights and freedoms, and the potentially abusive exercise of executive power. As many studies of these new democracies in particular seemed to indicate, popular and constitutional democracy were no longer necessarily bound together.

Thus, the important conceptual distinction between the popular and constitutional components of democracy has become more important in practice. And with this development comes also a relative weighting process, in which the popular element becomes downgraded with respect to the constitutional element. Once democracy is divided into its popular and constitutional elements, in other words, it is the popular that loses ground. For Zakaria, for example, who has always been one of the

2. See also the more recent discussions in Mény and Surel (2002), Dahl (1999), and Eisenstadt (1999).

clearest voices in this area, it is the presence of the constitutional rather than the popular component that is essential for the survival and well-being of democracy, and the reason democracy has proved so successful in the western hemisphere: 'For much of modern history, what characterized governments in Europe and North America, and differentiated them from those around the world, was not democracy but constitutional liberalism. The "Western model" is best symbolized not by the mass plebiscite but the impartial judge' (Zakaria, 1997: 27). In this view it is not elections – or not elections as such – that make for democracy, but rather the courts, or at least the combination of courts with other modes of non-electoral participation. Indeed, as some of the literature on good governance seems to imply with respect to the developing countries, a relatively clear formula is already available: NGOs (non-governmental organizations) + judges = democracy. While an emphasis on 'civil society' is acceptable, and reliance on legal procedures is indispensable, elections as such are not of the essence (see also Chua, 2003).

A similar logic can be seen in various approaches to constitutional reform in the advanced democracies and to reforms within the EU context in particular, in that here too democracy can be redefined in a way that downgrades the importance of its popular component. As Michelle Everson (2000: 106) has noted in her discussion of Majone's work, for example, 'non-majoritarian thought ... forcefully claims that its isolation of market governance from political forces serves the goal of democracy by safeguarding the democratically set goals of the polity from the predatory inclinations of a transitory political elite.' In this case the opposition is unequivocal: in one corner, the goals of the polity, objectively defined; in the other, the claims of a transitory – because elected – and hence predatory elite. The one is sustained by the networks of good governance, the other by the crude power and ambition of electoral politics. There is clearly no contest here. In other arenas, and in the context of different processes, the story appears the same. In their review of new modes of delegation, Mark Thatcher and Alec Stone Sweet (2003: 19) underline the growing importance of 'procedural legitimacy', which 'relies on a process of decision making by NMIs [non-majoritarian institutions] being better than the insular, often secret, deliberations of cabinets and executives'. In this case, the benefits of transparency, legality and stakeholder access are held up against the limits and distortions induced by partisan politics, and are seen to lead to a process offering 'a fair and democratic substitute for electoral accountability'. The shift becomes even more pronounced with the import of the modalities of New Public Management into political organizations and the public sector. Here, the forms of accountability not only do not include the electoral channel, but also override the criteria implicit in the public sector as such, being governed instead by values of cost-efficiency, fair procedure, and performance (see, for example, Peters, 2003: 125).

This, in turn, leads to a second puzzle: If democracy is being redefined to downgrade its popular component, then why is this happening, and why now? In other words, why did this particular shift begin to appear less that one decade after the much heralded 'victory of democracy' (e.g., Hadenius, 1997), and at a moment when, for the first time in history, democracy was being acclaimed as 'the only game in town' (Linz and Stepan, 1996)? Why, just as democracy seemed to triumph, did there emerge a concern to limit its scope?

There are, of course, a number of different but related answers to this question – including the impact of the

end of the Cold War, the decline of the 'embedded liberalism' that moderated the spontaneous tendencies of
the major capitalist economies for three decades after
1945,[3] the declining purchase of party government, and
the more general fallout from processes of globalization
and Europeanization. For now, however, I will focus on
one answer, and suggest that the shift from popular to
constitutional democracy and the concomitant downgrading of politics and of electoral processes are at least
partly the consequence of the failings of political parties.
As parties fail, so too fails popular democracy. Or, to
put it another way, thanks to the failings of parties,
popular democracy can no longer function in the way
in which we have come to understand and accept it, and
in the way it has always functioned up to now. In going
beyond parties, democracy also passes beyond popular
involvement and control.

REDEFINING DEMOCRACY

Some twenty years before *The Semi-Sovereign People*,
Schattschneider famously proposed that democracy
without parties was unthinkable. The phrase itself comes
from the opening paragraph of his *Party Government*
(1942: 1) and is worth citing in its full context:

> The rise of political parties is indubitably one of the prin-
> cipal distinguishing marks of modern government. The
> parties, in fact, have played a major role as *makers* of
> governments, more especially they have been the makers
> of democratic government. It should be stated flatly at
> the outset that this volume is devoted to the thesis that
> the political parties created democracy and that modern
> democracy is unthinkable save in terms of parties. As

---

3. For the notion of 'embedded liberalism', see further Ruggie
(1982). [*Ed.*]

a matter of fact, the condition of the parties is the best
possible evidence of the nature of any regime. The most
important distinction in modern political philosophy, the
distinction between democracy and dictatorship, can be
made best in terms of party politics. The parties are not
therefore merely appendages of modern government;
they are in the center of it and play a determinative and
creative role in it.

As always in the writings of this period, of course,
democracy in this case was both popular and constitutional; it was the democracy of elections as well as of
checks and balances, and the democracy of mandates,
popular accountability, and representative government. It was this all-embracing sense of democracy that
Schattschneider found unthinkable except in terms of
parties, and the sheer conviction of his opinion has led
to his proposition being cited by party specialists ever
since. Thus, for example, it is argued that despite all
the problems facing parties, and despite different and
cumulative challenges, they will continue to survive,
as Schattschneider suggests, as long as democracy sur-
vives. This is one of the key motifs in Russell Dalton
and Martin Wattenberg's assessment, which begins by
asking readers to 'think Schattschneider's unthinkable'
and to consider what might happen should parties fail,
and concludes on a more sanguine note by reaffirming
that 'it remains difficult to think of national governments functioning without parties playing a significant
role in connecting the various elements of the political process' (2000: 275). But if we take account of the
different components of democracy, and then think
Schattschneider's proposition through to its potentially
logical conclusion, we may arrive at a different answer.
In other words, while Schattschneider's proposition is
usually taken to mean that the survival of democracy
will guarantee the survival of parties (and since the

survival of democracy is guaranteed, this means that the survival of parties is also guaranteed), we can also read it the other way around, suggesting that the failure of parties might indeed imply the failure of democracy, or, adopting Dalton and Wattenberg's terms, that the failure of parties might imply at least the failure of modern (representative) government. If democracy, or representative government, is unthinkable save in terms of parties, then perhaps, in the face of party failings, it does indeed become unthinkable, or unworkable.

Without parties, and still following Schattschneider, we are then left either with no real democracy and no real system of representative government, or with what is still called democracy, now redefined so as to downgrade or even exclude the popular component – since it is this component that depends so closely on party. Without parties, in other words, we are left with a stripped-down version of constitutional or Madisonian democracy; or we are left with other post-popular versions of democracy, such as Pettit's republican polity (1998: 303), or those systems of modern governance that seek to combine 'stakeholder participation' with 'problem-solving efficiency' (Kohler-Koch, 2005). These are certainly not unthinkable forms of polity, but they are systems in which conventional popular democracy plays little or no significant role, and in which neither elections nor parties remain privileged.

When democracy in Schattschneider's terms becomes unthinkable, in short, other modes of democracy move to the fore. Hence the contemporary intellectual interest in the theory of democratic renewal, and hence the more practical interest – represented by Amy Chua and Fareed Zakaria, among others – in proposing new forms of institutional politics. These and other similar approaches share a common concern to find or define a notion of democracy that, first of all, works; second, is accepted as legitimate; and yet, third, no longer places at its centre the notion of popular control or electoral accountability.

But in what sense are we without parties, and in what sense are they failing? My argument is that they are failing in two related ways, and I will go on to look at these at greater length. First, as is now well established, parties are increasingly failing in their capacity to engage ordinary citizens, who are voting in smaller numbers than before and with less sense of partisan consistency, and are also increasingly reluctant to commit themselves to parties, whether in terms of identification or membership. In this sense, citizens are withdrawing from conventional political involvement. Second, the parties can no longer adequately serve as a base for the activities and status of their own leaders, who increasingly direct their ambitions towards external public institutions and draw their resources from them. Parties may provide a necessary platform for political leaders, but this is increasingly the sort of platform that is used as a stepping stone to other offices and positions. Parties are failing, in other words, as a result of a process of mutual withdrawal or abandonment, whereby citizens retreat into private life or into more specialized and often ad hoc forms of representation, while the party leaderships retreat into the institutions, drawing their terms of reference ever more readily from their roles as governors or public-office holders. Parties are failing because the zone of engagement – the traditional world of party democracy where citizens interacted with and felt a sense of attachment to their political leaders – is being evacuated.

1

THE PASSING OF POPULAR INVOLVEMENT

In this chapter I focus on the evidence of popular withdrawal and disengagement from conventional politics and discuss the emptying of the space in which citizen interaction with political representatives might be expected to be at its closest and most active. This is a relatively familiar process, which has already been dealt with, sometimes in greater detail, in the scholarly literature as well as in more popular commentaries. However, what is often missing from those treatments is the awareness of just how pervasive and wide-ranging the process actually is. Moreover, while some aspects of popular withdrawal have received ample attention, others have not, and hence the whole gamut of features has not been brought together in one overall and accessible assessment. This chapter aims to do that, and to indicate the breadth and variety of the modes of disengagement, even if some of these are clearly less substantial than others. Here and elsewhere in this book, I assume that withdrawal and disengagement are symptomatic of a growing indifference to conventional politics – that is, they are symptomatic of indifference to politics with a capital *P*, which may not mean indifference to Beck's 'sub-politics' (Beck, 1992)[1] I also want to show here that this indifference is evident on both sides of the democratic bridge. That is, I am concerned to emphasize the evidence of indifference on the part of both the citizenry *and* the political class: they are withdrawing and disengaging from one another, and it is in this sense that there is an emptying of the space in which citizens and their representatives interact.

Party democracy, which would normally offer a point of connection and site of engagement for citizens and their political leaders, is being enfeebled, with the result that elections and the electoral process become little more than 'dignified' parts of the modern democratic constitution. That is, elections have less and less practical effect, because the working, or 'efficient' part of the constitution is being steadily relocated elsewhere (Katz and Mair, 1995: 22).[2] This enfeeblement is expressed by citizen withdrawal from active engagement in, and commitment to, conventional political life, on the one hand, and by the retreat of political leaders into the institutions of the state, on the other. This process has had two notable concomitants, which should be mentioned right away. First, in terms of politics on the ground, the

---

1. Indeed, for some authors, including Beck, withdrawal from capital-P politics is often believed to be compensated for by greater involvement in 'sub-politics'. Note also W. Lance Bennett's (1998: 744) suggestion that 'what is changing about politics is not a decline in citizen engagement, but a shift away from old forms that is complemented by the emergence of new forms of political interest and engagement ... [C]ivic culture is not dead; it has merely taken new identities, and can be found living in other communities.' Whether such relocation of involvement can compensate for disengagement from conventional politics is a major question.

2. For the original distinction between the dignified and efficient parts of the constitution, see Bagehot (1963: 61).

widening gap between rulers and ruled has facilitated the often strident populist challenge that is now a feature of many advanced European democracies – the challenge represented by the far-right People's or Progress parties in Denmark and Norway, by Strache and Wilders in Austria and the Netherlands, De Winter and Le Pen in Flanders and France, and by Blocher and Bossi in Switzerland and Italy. Each of these particular versions of the challenge to the political mainstream has its own nationally specific set of ideas, policies and interests, often revolving around shared expressions of xenophobia, racism and cultural defence, and usually emerging on the right wing of the political spectrum (Mudde, 2008). But each is also marked by a common and often very explicit hostility to what is seen in the different countries as the national political class. In other words, I argue that because of the gap that has been created by the process of mutual withdrawal, and really for the first time in postwar political history, the political class itself has now become a matter of contention in a large number of democratic polities.

The second concomitant – in part a cause of the withdrawal and in part a consequence – operates at the level of public policy, and may be seen in the growing acceptability and legitimation of non-political, or depoliticized, modes of decision-making. Among the important manifestations of this tendency are the growing significance (in both range and weight) of so-called 'non-majoritarian institutions'; the growing importance of the European Union as a decision-making forum, and, on a wider stage, the greater weight accorded to other supranational and international agencies, including the World Trade Organization and International Monetary Fund, the Association of South-East Asian Nations, and so on; the increasing tendency for citizens and politicians to seek redress for grievances and problems through judicial or quasi-judicial solutions; and the growing acceptance that the modern state is regulatory in character, and hence limited in its capacities, rather than political or redistributive.

In sum, because of the growing enfeeblement of party democracy, and the indifference towards party democracy that is being expressed on both sides of the political divide, we now find ourselves being offered as alternative scenarios either the populist or the ostensibly non-political expert.[3]

CITIZEN DISENGAGEMENT

Although concern about citizen disengagement from conventional politics is now more and more frequently expressed, both in the scholarly literature and in the popular media, the evidence of this withdrawal is sometimes disputed. It is also quite scattered, making an encompassing picture more difficult to sketch. A major purpose of this chapter is therefore to bring together the disparate sets of evidence with a view to underlining the degree of coherence and consistency they reflect. Indeed, one of the reasons this evidence, or, more properly, the weight of this evidence, is sometimes disputed, is that the different elements are seen in isolation from one another. The fact that levels of participation in national elections do not always register a sharp or very steady decline, for example, is sometimes cited as evidence of a continuing popular commitment to conventional

---

3. Occasionally, and in this context the Dutch Pim Fortuyn offered an excellent example, we get both. That is, we get a populist political leader such as Prof Dr Fortuyn, who was backed up by a team composed of supposed experts, often with hands-on experience in the organization of different policy areas, and whose appeal was based on offering practical solutions derived from knowledge and expertise rather than political or ideological preference.

politics, even though the small changes that do occur in this regard are often consistent with other trends that appear to underline a wide-scale pattern of withdrawal. In other words, even a small decline in, say, the level of turnout at elections, may be seen to weigh more heavily when placed in the context of other equivalent shifts in mass political behaviour.

In fact, what we see here are two features that are not normally seen to be applicable to changes at the level of mass politics in Europe. The first is that virtually all of these separate pieces of evidence point in the same direction. This in itself is very unusual. Analysts of data relating to mass politics almost invariably expect to find mutually opposing trends in the different streams of indicators – that is, while one indicator might point in one direction, it is often contradicted by a second indicator pointing in a different direction. Mass politics rarely moves in concert, but in this case it is precisely the consistency of the trends that is striking. Second, virtually all of these trends in the data are consistent across countries. This again is most unusual. The normal expectation in comparative political research is that while particular trends in mass politics may well be noted in some countries, they are almost never pervasive. Some countries may shift together, but it is only very rarely that all, or even most, shift in the same way and at the same time. What we see now, however, is a much clearer indication of cross-national convergence in the trends that matter. In other words, not only are these various trends now pointing in the same direction, they are also doing so almost everywhere.

ELECTORAL PARTICIPATION

So what trends are we talking about here? Let me begin with the most obvious and most immediate indicator: the level of participation in national elections. Given what has been said about citizen withdrawal in the more popular media in particular, it is by means of this indicator that we might expect some of the most striking trends to be identified. At the same time, however, it is often this particular evidence that is most strongly disputed. In other words, while various expectations regarding the possible decline in levels of electoral turnout have been current for some years, they have often been found to have little backing in the aggregate empirical data. Reviewing the evidence from the 1960s through to the end of the 1980s, for example, Rudy Andeweg (1996: 150–51) noted that most countries in Europe were exhibiting more or less trendless fluctuation in turnout levels: although participation rates among those eligible to vote had indeed fallen in some countries in this thirty-year period, they had increased in others, resulting in what was in fact just a very small decline in Europe as a whole across this period. Taking a much larger set of countries, and looking at data running through to a later date, Pippa Norris also found little or no evidence of serious decline. Among the advanced, postindustrial democracies, turnout as a percentage of the voting age population rose during the 1950s, stabilized in the 1960s, 1970s and 1980s, and then underwent what Norris refers to as 'a modest slippage' in the 1990s. This slight fall was statistically insignificant, however, leaving a more generalized pattern among the majority of nations of 'trendless fluctuation or stability' (Norris, 2002: 54–55, 67). Another assessment, by Mark Franklin (2002), was also inclined to dismiss any real concern. Franklin noted that although turnout in the long-established democracies might have declined at the end of the century, this was usually only relative to the very high levels recorded in the 1960s, and was probably reflecting simply a short-term lack of interest in contingently quite non-divisive contests: 'elections in recent years may see lower turnout for the simple reason that these elections decide issues of lesser importance than elections did in the late 1950s' (2002: 164). Once more important issues were at stake, he implied, participation levels could be expected to increase again. If, of course, these important issues never materialized – as I argue is the most likely scenario, given the decline of party democracy – then turnout might never pick up. Elsewhere, in a very extensive and precise analysis, Franklin (2004) linked the slight decline in turnout to the effects of generational replacement: turnout falls because non-participating younger people replace participatory older generations in ever-changing electorates. In this case, it is not so much that existing citizens withdraw or disengage, as that younger citizens, whose demographic weight naturally increases with time, were never engaged to begin with.

Whatever the reasons for any fall in levels of participation, therefore, these analyses seem mainly quite sanguine about the trends. Long-term stability in levels of participation has been followed by a slight decline, but this is not so great that it need be a source of worry for those concerned with the healthy functioning of modern democratic life. Is this a reasonable conclusion? On the face of it, and especially with regard to the European data, the interpretation is certainly plausible.[4] Thus, through each of the four decades from the 1950s to the 1980s, average turnout levels in western Europe scarcely altered, increasing marginally from 84.3 per

4. For details of the figures reported here, see Mair (2002), from which the discussion of the aggregate indicators is largely drawn.

cent in the 1950s to 84.9 per cent in the 1960s, and then falling slightly to 83.9 per cent in the 1970s and to 81.7 per cent in the 1980s. This was essentially the steady-state period, as has been emphasized by Norris and Franklin. That said, the decline from the 1970s to the 1980s, while small, was remarkably consistent across fifteen long-established European democracies, with just three countering an otherwise general trend: in Belgium, where voting is compulsory, turnout increased slightly from 92.9 to 93.9 per cent from the 1970s to the 1980s; in Norway, where turnout increased from 81.6 to 83.1 per cent; and in the Netherlands, where mean turnout remained more or less unchanged. In each of the other twelve countries for which long-term data are available, however, mean levels did in fact decline in the 1980s, whether marginally, as in Austria, which recorded a fall of less than 1 per cent, or more substantially, as in France, which recorded a fall of more than 10 per cent. The decline may have been marginal when looked at cross-nationally, but it was almost universal, and hence might well have justified some concern.

More important, it is a trend that began to accelerate in the 1990s and beyond, with average turnout across western Europe falling from 81.7 per cent to 77.6 per cent in the last decade of the twentieth century, and to 75.8 in the first decade of the new century. To be sure, even at this level, which is the lowest recorded in any of the postwar decades, turnout remained relatively high, with an average of slightly more than three-quarters of national electorates casting a ballot in the elections held during the 1990s, a figure that remains substantially higher than that recorded in nationwide elections in the United States, for example. Even allowing for this, however, and for the fact that the drop from the 1980s to the 2000s is little more than 6 per cent, it is nevertheless striking to see the overall European figure in the 1990s dipping below the 80 per cent level for the first time in five decades. Here also, moreover, there is a striking consistency across countries, in that, looking back from the turn of the century, eleven of the fifteen democracies involved also recorded their lowest ever decade averages in those ten years. The exceptions to this pattern again include Belgium, where the decade averages are almost invariant, but where the lowest level was recorded in the 1960s, and Denmark and Sweden, which both recorded their lowest levels in the 1950s. Even in these three cases, however, it should be noted that the average level of turnout in the 1990s was lower than in the 1980s. The fourth exception is the United Kingdom, which was unusual in recording its trough in participation in the 1980s. Indeed, the UK is the only one of these fifteen countries that recorded even a marginally higher level of turnout in the 1990s than in the 1980s, although in this case turnout later plunged to a remarkable low of just 59 per cent in the first election of the twenty-first century.

This pattern is therefore very striking, and all the more so when account is taken of the sheer extent of the decline in particular countries. In Austria, for example, where turnout had remained safely above the 90 per cent level in each of the preceding four decades, the drop in the 1990s was almost 8 per cent. Similarly sharp declines were recorded in Finland, in Germany, which had absorbed the new voters of the former Democratic Republic during this period, and in the Netherlands and Norway. Even more striking, although across the longer term, is the case of Switzerland, where the then exclusively male electorate recorded an average of 69 per cent turnout in the 1950s – higher than that recorded in France or Ireland during the 1990s – but which, this time with equal rights for women, recorded an average of less than 44 per cent in the 1990s. In other words, more and more countries experienced record low decade averages in the 1990s, these in some cases reflecting very sharp declines.

This trend has persisted into the twenty-first century. As noted, the 2001 election in the UK was marked by the lowest level of turnout since the advent of mass democracy. The 2002 parliamentary elections in both France and Ireland were also marked by historic low levels of turnout, and while Ireland picked up again in 2007, France fell to a new record low of 60.4 per cent. Record lows were also recorded in 2008 in Italy and 2001 in Norway, as well as in 2002 in Portugal, and in 2000 in Spain. Levels close to historic lows were recorded in Greece in 2000, in Switzerland in 2003, in Austria in 2006 and in Finland in 2007. Why the trend towards ever lower levels of participation has continued remains, of course, an open question, to which we will return. It may simply reflect generational shifts. It may also be because of sheer boredom. The key point, however, is that we are seeing something that is both unidirectional and pervasive, and that offers a striking indicator of the growing enfeeblement of the electoral process.

There is one other way of seeing this picture that is perhaps even more telling. Indicators of turnout change are somewhat like those of climate change: the shifts we see do not necessarily occur in great leaps or bounds, and are not always linear. Moreover, while indicating withdrawal and disengagement, change in turnout levels is often registered as a trickle rather than a flood. For these reasons, and again like the indicators of climate change, the importance of what is often just a slight or uneven trend may be underestimated or even disputed. One way in which climatologists get around this problem is by laying less stress on the trends as such, and by drawing attention instead to the patterns that are visible in the timing and frequency of the peak values. This is, in fact, a very simple approach to measurement, and is also intuitively meaningful. Thus, for example, in a publication from 2003, Phil Jones and Anders Moberg adduced clear evidence of global warming by noting that the warmest decade on record had been the most recent, the 1990s, while 1998 emerged as the warmest single year, followed by 2001. Further evidence of global warming was adduced by noting that the eight warmest years on record had all occurred since 1990, even though in that same period air temperatures were also recorded (for example, in 1992, 1993 and 1994) that were little higher than those reached in the late 1970s. In other words, the pattern is evident, even if the trend is not wholly unidirectional.

The same is true for turnout levels, and indeed for many other indicators of mass political behaviour, and for this reason the sheer extent of change at this level is also often underestimated. Although there is no undisturbed downward trend in levels of electoral participation, for example, record lows now come with greater frequency, and in a greater number of polities. As can be seen from Table 1(a) overleaf, which lists the three elections with the lowest levels of turnout in each of the fifteen long-established European democracies, almost four-fifths of these elections have taken place since 1990. In other words, not only do the last decades hold the record for the lowest turnout of any postwar decade in western Europe, but within the great majority of west European democracies, most, or even all of the record low turnouts have occurred since 1990. The two clearest exceptions are Denmark and Sweden, where, seemingly for unremarkable contingent reasons, the lowest-turnout elections fell in the 1950s. Beyond these cases, the only other odd exceptions are one low-turnout election in the 1960s (in Belgium), another one in the 1970s (again in Belgium), and two in the 1980s

Table 1 Record low levels of turnout in western Europe, 1950–2009

(a) Years of lowest turnout

Austria	1994, 1999, 2006
Belgium	1968, 1974, 1999
Denmark	1950, 1953 (i), 1953 (ii)
Finland	1991, 1999, 2007
France	1988, 2002, 2007
Germany	1990, 1994, 2005
Iceland	1999, 2007, 2009
Ireland	1997, 2002, 2007
Italy	1996, 2001, 2008
Luxembourg	1989, 1994, 1999
Netherlands	1994, 1998, 2002
Norway	1993, 2001, 2005
Sweden	1952, 1956, 1958
Switzerland	1995, 1999, 2003
UK	1997, 2001, 2005

(b) Frequency of record low turnouts, by decade

	No.	%
1950–59	6	13.3
1960–69	1	2.2
1970–79	1	2.2
1980–89	2	4.4
1990–99	18	40.0
2000–09	17	37.8

(in France and Luxembourg). The remaining thirty-five cases all date from 1990 or later. In other words, however small the overall shifts in turnout might be, they are nevertheless clustering together in a remarkable fashion – see Table 1(b). Indeed, this pattern also extends to the newer southern European democracies: the three lowest levels of turnout recorded in post-authoritarian Greece were those in 1996, 2000 and 2007; in Portugal, the lowest levels were recorded in 1999, 2002 and 2005; and in Spain in two of the three lowest turnouts fell in 1989 and 2000 (the third was in 1979). Here, as in the long-established democracies, the more recent the elections, the more likely they are to record troughs in participation. There is no certainty here, of course; like the pattern evinced by climate change, turnout sometimes bucks the overall trend, even today. However, the overall direction and reach of the change is unmistakable, and it offers the first strong indicator of the increase in popular withdrawal and disengagement from conventional politics.[5]

ELECTORAL VOLATILITY

The second key aggregate indicator relates to the behaviour of those citizens who do participate, and measures the extent to which their voting patterns reveal consistency and stability over time in the distribution of partisan preferences. Those citizens who continue to vote in elections are clearly still engaged with conventional politics, however marginally. As popular involvement fades, however, and as indifference grows, we can expect that even these citizens who do continue to participate will prove more volatile, more uncertain and more random in their expressions of preference. If politics no longer counts for so much, then not only should the willingness to vote begin to falter; so also should the sense of commitment among those who continue to take part. Choices are likely to prove more fickle, and to be more susceptible to the play of short-term factors. In practice, this also means that election outcomes are likely to prove less and less predictable. Electoral volatility is likely to increase; new parties and or new candidates are likely to prove more successful; and traditional alignments are likely to come under pressure. Hand in hand with indifference goes inconsistency.

---

5. For a comparable conclusion with reference to data from the American case, see Thomas E. Paterson (2002).

As with patterns in turnout, expectations of growing unpredictability in the balance of party support in national party systems in western Europe have been current for a number of years. Here too, however, the empirical record at the aggregate level has usually failed to confirm them. Thus while party systems in some countries did indeed experience a substantial increase in their levels of electoral flux through the 1970s and 1980s, others appeared to become even more settled than before, resulting in what was generally a 'stable' and relatively subdued level of aggregate electoral change across western Europe as a whole (Bartolini and Mair, 1990). For many observers, such findings proved puzzling, since the evidence from survey data in particular had suggested that in the 1970s the western democracies had already begun to experience symptoms of breakdown in their traditional electoral alignments and historic cleavage voting patterns (Dalton et al., 1983; Franklin et al., 1992). As it turned out, however, these undeniable changes at the level of individual behaviour did not seem to translate into equivalent shifts in the party balance at the aggregate level. Indeed, even by the end of the 1980s, aggregate electoral volatility on a European-wide basis remained relatively muted, while many of the traditional parties that had already dominated electoral competition in the 1950s or even earlier continued to be serious contenders. These older parties had certainly seen some of their aggregate support slipping away to the benefit of new formations, but even by the end of the 1980s it was striking to see how much of their overall vote share they managed to retain.

This is borne out by the mean levels of aggregate electoral volatility in the period from 1950s to the 1980s. The measure applied here is that originally proposed by Mogens Pedersen (1979), who calculated the level of volatility simply by summing the (aggregate) electoral gains of all winning parties in a given election, or, which is the same thing, the (aggregate) electoral losses of all losing parties. It is, of course, a crude aggregate measure, and it may well underestimate the real level of vote switching – as measured by individual survey evidence, or whatever. As an aggregate measure, however, it has the advantage of being calculable for all elections, including those in the distant past as well as those in polities where survey data are either absent or unreliable. In any case, the point here is to note that by this measure, contrary to many expectations, levels of aggregate electoral volatility across the fifteen long-standing democracies in Europe scarcely changed between the 1950s and the 1980s: the west European national average fell from 7.9 per cent in the 1950s to 6.9 per cent in the 1960s, and then rose to just 8.9 per cent in the 1970s and in the 1980s. This was hardly the stuff of electoral earthquakes. That said, these averages did conceal quite a bit of flux within the individual party systems. Denmark, the Netherlands and Norway moved from remarkably quiet elections in the 1950s to relatively unstable elections in the 1970s, before returning again to more stable outcomes in the 1980s. In contrast, both France and Germany began the postwar period marked by the substantial flux of postwar political reconstruction, and then settled down to more steady-state politics in the 1960s and 1970s. In other words, while the average level of aggregate electoral volatility in western Europe as a whole tended to remain quite stable, this was partly masking the contradictory patterns in the experiences of the different polities.

Here again, however, as with the evidence of turnout, the more important observation is that this picture began to change significantly in the 1990s. Across western Europe as a whole, the 1990s became the peak decade for electoral volatility, with a score of 12.6 per cent, almost 4 points higher than that recorded in the 1970s and 1980s. Not too much should be made of this, of course. On a scale with a theoretical range running from 0 to 100, and which even here had a range of decade averages that ran in practice from 2.5 (1950s Switzerland) to 22.9 (1990s Italy), a mean value of 12.6 still reflects more (short-term) stability than change. On the other hand, the 1990s was the first of the five postwar decades in which the overall mean of instability breached 10 per cent, and also the first decade to record such a major shift from the previous mean value.

The significance of the 1990s is also underlined by reference to the individual national experiences. In all but four of the countries (the exceptions are Denmark, France, Germany and Luxembourg), the 1990s consti- tuted a new national peak in volatility levels, which, in the majority of cases, easily exceeded 10 per cent: 10.8 in Belgium, 11.0 in Finland, 13.7 in Iceland, 11.7 in Ireland, 22.9 in Italy, 19.1 in the Netherlands, 15.8 in Norway and 13.8 in Sweden. Indeed, of all the individual national elections held in the 1990s, close to two-thirds recorded volatility levels in above 10 per cent. This con- fluence was also unprecedented, and again signalled that the patterns at the end of the century were markedly dif- ferent from those of the earlier postwar years.

Moreover, and as with the turnout data, there was little sign that these new excesses had begun to abate in the new century. In elections in 2002, both Austria and the Netherlands experienced record high levels of aggregate instability, as did Italy in 2001. France, Norway and Sweden also recorded remarkably high levels of volatility in their first twenty-first-century elec- tions, although in these cases no absolute records were broken. More generally, as can be seen in Table 2, a clear majority of the most unstable national elections to be recorded since 1950 have occurred since 1990.

Table 2 Record high levels of volatility in western Europe, 1950–2009

(a) Years of highest volatility

Austria	1994, 2002, 2008
Belgium	1965, 1981, 2003
Denmark	1973, 1975, 1977
Finland	1970, 1991, 1995
France	1955, 1958, 2002
Germany	1953, 1961, 1990
Iceland	1978, 1999, 2009
Ireland	1951, 1987, 1992
Italy	1992, 1994, 2001
Luxembourg	1954, 1984, 1989
Netherlands	1994, 2002, 2006
Norway	1997, 2001, 2005
Sweden	1991, 1998, 2006
Switzerland	1991, 1999, 2003
UK	1974(i), 1979, 1997

(b) Frequency of elections with record high volatility, by decade

	No.	%
1950–59	5	11.1
1960–69	2	4.4
1970–79	7	15.6
1980–89	4	8.8
1990–99	15	33.3
2000–09	12	26.7

The very simple approach to presenting the data here is again borrowed from the climatologists, and follows the breakdown applied to the turnout data in Table 1. In this case the pattern is not so one-sided: volatility data inevitably prove more erratic than turnout data, being quickly responsive to political crises as well as to institutional and social-structural change (Bartolini and Mair, 1990: 253–308). Nevertheless, the period since 1990 again proves exceptional: not only do 60 per cent of the record national highs in volatility fall in this period – one-third in the 1990s, more than a quarter in the next ten years – but it is also noteworthy that no other decade comes close to matching this clustering. Indeed, in no earlier decade does the number of high volatility elections even come close to double figures. Once again, the more recent the elections, the less likely they are to yield a predictable outcome.

Since 1990, in short, ever fewer voters have seemed ready to participate in elections, although turnout levels in themselves have remained reasonably high, while among those who do participate, there has been a greater likelihood that they will switch their preferences from one election to the next.[6] Not only has each of these indicators reached a relative extreme in the period since 1990 (whether recording troughs in turnout, or peaks in volatility) across western Europe as a whole, they also tend to the extreme in a large majority of the individual polities. That is, *both* extreme lows in turnout *and* extreme peaks in volatility have been recorded since 1990 in almost all of the long-established European democracies. The exceptions were Luxembourg, which had very low turnout but only moderate volatility; Sweden, which recorded high volatility but not exceptionally low turnout; and Denmark, which proved extreme on neither indicator during this recent period. Beyond these cases, the evidence of unusual patterns since 1990 is not only striking, but also remarkably consistent. Across western Europe, citizens, where they are not abstaining from the ballot altogether, are voting with significantly reduced partisan commitment. In these heightened levels of instability, we see a second strong aggregate indicator of disengagement.

---

6. This counters an earlier observation by Bennett, based on the US data (1998: 745). Even though conventional political participation may be in decline, he suggested, 'those who continue to participate in traditional politics exhibit stability and substance in electoral choice, opinion formation, and policy deliberation'. To judge by the west European data, it is clear they do not.

PARTY LOYALTIES

The same message comes through more and more clearly from individual-level survey data. That is, the often substantial shifts evinced by these aggregate data on turnout and volatility now correspond closely to the evidence of individual-level experiences as tapped by election studies and commercial polling projects. Many of these latter data have been collated and summarized by Dalton and Wattenberg in their comprehensive *Parties Without Partisans* (2000), and what is also striking in this instance is both the consistency and the pervasiveness of the various changes that have been observed. One key indicator is the degree to which individual voters feel a sense of belonging or commitment to particular political parties, a feeling captured by various measures of partisan identification. And here (Table 3) decline is very evident: in eleven of the thirteen countries,

Table 3 Trends in party identification in western Europe, 1960s–1990s

| | Per annum trend in: | |
Country	% party identifiers	% strong party identifiers
Austria	–0.916	–0.663
Belgium	+0.090	–0.285
UK	–0.202	–0.882
Denmark	+0.001	–0.207
Finland	–0.293	–0.147
France	–0.712	–0.329
Iceland	–0.675	–0.250
Ireland	–1.510	–0.767
Italy	–0.979	–0.770
Luxembourg	–0.317	–0.316
Netherlands	–0.329	–0.129
Norway	–0.542	–0.450
Sweden	–0.733	–0.543

Source: Dalton (2004: 33), as derived from Eurobarometer and election study data.

including a number of non–European Union polities, for which relevant data are available – the exceptions are Belgium and Denmark – the percentage of voters claiming a sense of identification with parties has fallen over the past two decades or so. Even more strikingly, the smaller numbers of voters who report a strong sense of belonging or identification has also decidedly fallen, and this time in every single one of the countries concerned. As Dalton notes, it is not just the scale of the decline that is important here, but also the fact that it occurs in all of the cases for which data are available. There therefore seems little that is either contingent or circumstantial, and as with so many other data discussed in this chapter, 'the similarity in trends for so many nations forces us to look beyond specific and idiosyncratic explanations ... For public opinion trends to be so consistent across so many nations, something broader and deeper must be occurring' (Dalton, 2000: 29).

Yet more evidence of this broader and deeper process can be seen in the other sets of survey data that Dalton and his colleagues marshal. Split-ticket voting, for example, whereby voters opt for one party in one electoral arena, and for another party in another electoral arena, has risen in all those cases where it can be measured over time (Australia, Canada, Germany, Sweden and the United States). A committed and engaged voter, with strong partisan loyalty, will normally vote for the same party regardless of the arena involved – for example, voting Democrat in US presidential and congressional contests, as well as probably in local state and county elections. Lesser partisan commitment and lesser engagement are more likely to be associated with more free-range voting patterns, and hence with a greater willingness to split the ticket, and it is this latter practice that is growing. Voters are also less ready or less able to decide in advance how they will vote, preferring to observe the campaign, or even remaining uninterested, until closer to polling day. Here too, with a single Danish exception, this pattern is more and more prevalent, with almost every election study reporting a substantial increase in the proportion of voters who make their decision how to vote either during the campaign or only shortly before polling day. Again, the implication is a lack of stable commitment on the part of voters, and hence also a lack of engagement. It is also hardly surprising, then, to see that these voters are also far less likely to engage in more demanding campaign activities, whether this might be by way of attending political meetings, working for a party or candidate, persuading others to vote in a particular way, or even donating money. On almost all of these measures, and in almost all the countries for which data are available, the survey evidence once again clearly points to decline: individual voters are less and less willing to participate in this more demanding sense – for many, at least as far as conventional politics is concerned, it is enough to be simply spectators.

PARTY MEMBERSHIP

Citizens are also obviously much less willing to take on the obligations and commitments associated with membership in party organizations. Here too, it is striking to note not only the sheer decline in the number of party members over time, but also the extent to which this decline seems characteristic of all long-established democracies (Van Biezen et al., 2009). Although the pattern here is more pronounced than in the case of changes in levels of turnout or of electoral volatility, the conclusions that have been drawn about party membership levels tend to reiterate in an even more compelling way those drawn about the more conventional levels of participation. In other words, through to the 1980s, the evidence of decline in this form of political engagement was somewhat ambiguous and disputable. From the 1990s onwards, by contrast, the trend has been unequivocal and seemingly unstoppable.

The first major study based on aggregate – often official party – data was that summarized in Katz and Mair (1992), and covered a large number of European polities from the beginning of the 1960s through to the end of the 1980s. This study found that, while there was a decline in the numbers of party members as a proportion of their respective national electorates (the only exceptions were the cases of Belgium and West Germany), which were themselves expanding substantially in the population booms of this period, there was little evidence of decline in the actual numbers themselves. Indeed, by the end of the 1980s, it appeared that party membership had actually grown in absolute terms not only in Belgium and West Germany, but also in Sweden, Norway and Italy, while falling both in absolute terms and as a share of the electorate in Finland, the Netherlands, Austria, Denmark and the UK. A mixed picture, in other words, and one that led at the time to the conclusion that, contrary to prevailing expectations, there had been no wholesale 'collapse' in membership (Katz and Mair, 1992: 332). This conclusion was supported by a study that incorporated much of the available individual-level survey evidence on the topic (Widfeldt, 1995), and later again by a comparison of World Values Study survey data from the early 1980s and early 1990s. Indeed, far from seeing the party membership ratio entering a general decline through to the early 1990s, this latter analysis suggested that it had actually grown, and sometimes quite substantially, in such countries as Finland, Iceland, the Netherlands, Belgium, Norway, Britain and France. There seemed little evidence from these particular data that these countries were experiencing 'a spreading disillusionment with partisan politics' (Norris, 2002: 134, 135). On the contrary, the picture was one of vibrancy and engagement.

This relatively sanguine picture was shattered by the end of the 1990s. By then, and regardless of whatever conclusions might have been drawn from the survey data, the patterns in the aggregate data had become unequivocal. The first real check of the new patterns was reported in Mair and van Biezen (2001), and included data on thirteen long-established European democracies, as well as a number of the newer democracies. In each of the established cases, it turned out that the ratio of party membership to the electorate at large had fallen markedly between the beginning of the 1980s and the end of the 1990s (see also Scarrow [in Dalton], 2002: 86–95). That is, in not one of these cases had the membership ratio remained steady, let alone increased. The summary figures were truly striking: In 1980, an average of 9.8 per cent of the electorates in these thirteen long-established democracies were party members; by the end of the 1990s, the figure had fallen to just 5.7 per cent. To put it another way, and to trace the contrast back even further, at the beginning of the 1960s there were ten democracies in Europe for which it is possible to trace reliable membership figures, and across all ten the average membership ratio was 14 per cent; in a majority – six out of ten – of the countries, the ratio was above 10 per cent. In other words, more than one in every ten eligible voters were members of political parties. At the end of the 1990s, by contrast, there were twenty countries for which it was possible to find reliable membership data, some old democracies, some new. Across all twenty, the average membership ratio was just 5 per cent, little more than a third of the level recorded in the early 1960s, and of these twenty countries, only one – Austria – recorded a ratio exceeding 10 per cent.[7]

This evidence of uniform decline was also reinforced by the figures for the absolute numbers of party members, for here too, and in marked contrast to the earlier pattern noted by Katz and Mair (1992), the fall-off was pervasive: in every one of the long-established democracies included in the analysis, the absolute numbers of party members had fallen, sometimes by as much as 50 per cent of the 1980s levels. In no single country had there been an increase in the number of party members. This was exit on a grand scale – both in terms of reach and direction. Throughout the old democracies, as the analysis concluded, parties were simply haemorrhaging members (Mair and van Biezen, 2001: 13). In so doing, they offered yet another telling indicator of the extent to which the 1990s had been marked by an unprecedented degree of popular withdrawal and disengagement.

This story also continued into the new century. Though the levels of party membership in absolute numbers now appear to be bottoming out – indeed, they have often fallen so low as to make it almost impossible to imagine further decline in absolute numbers without this signalling the wholesale collapse of the party organizations concerned – the scale of the decline since the high point reached in the late 1970s is unmistakable. Table 4 shows a picture of membership loss of quite staggering

---

7. The pattern is comparable in the advanced democracies outside Europe. In Australia in 1967 there were 251,000 members, the equivalent of 4.1 per cent of the electorate; in 1997, the number had fallen to 231,000, equivalent to just 1.9 per cent of the then much expanded electorate – see the figures in McAllister (2002: 389–90); in Canada, the fall-off was from 462,000 members in 1987 to 372,000 in 1994, or from 2.6 per cent of the electorate to 1.9 per cent – see Carty (2002: 355); in New Zealand, the decline was from 272,000 (or 12.5 per cent) in 1981 to 133,000 (or 4.8 per cent) in 1999 – see Vowles (2002: 416–19).

proportions. A decline in the ratio of members to eligible voters is evident in each of the long-established democracies, ranging from a fall of more than 10 percentage points in the cases of Austria and Norway to more moderate decreases of around 2 or 3 per cent in Germany and the Netherlands. In the thirteen countries for which long-term data are available, the average membership ratio has fallen by nearly 5 percentage points in the last thirty years – a huge decline. The absolute numbers have also fallen dramatically. In the United Kingdom and France, the parties have lost around 1 million members over the course of the last three decades, equivalent to approximately two-thirds of the memberships recorded around 1980. Italian parties today have 1.5 million members fewer than their counterparts of the First Republic, corresponding to a fall by more than one-third of the earlier memberships. The Scandinavian countries too, and

Table 4 Party membership change in established democracies, 1980–2009

Country	Change in ratio of members to electorate	Change in number of members	% change in number of members
United Kingdom	−2.82	−1,118,274	−66.05
Norway	−10.20	−284,603	−61.75
France	−3.31	−974,475	−56.09
Sweden	−4.54	−241,130	−47.46
Ireland	−2.97	−50,856	−44.67
Switzerland	−5.90	−178,000	−43.22
Finland	−7.66	−260,261	−42.86
Denmark	−3.17	−109,467	−39.70
Italy	−4.09	−1,450,623	−35.61
Belgium	−3.45	−191,133	−30.97
Austria	−11.21	−422,661	−28.61
Netherlands	−1.77	−121,499	−28.19
Germany	−2.22	−531,856	−27.20
Portugal	−1.05	+4,306	+1.28
Greece	+3.40	+335,000	+148.89
Spain	+3.16	+1,208,258	+374.60

Source: Van Biezen et al. (2009)

Norway and Sweden in particular, have suffered severe losses, with the raw numbers falling by over 60 per cent and nearly 50 per cent respectively. Although the losses appear more muted in some countries, it should also be noted that in none of the established democracies have the raw memberships fallen by less than 25 per cent. On average, across all established democracies, membership levels in absolute numbers have been nearly halved since 1980.

CONCLUSION

So what can we conclude from this review of the evidence regarding citizen behaviour in western Europe? The most obvious conclusion is that it has now become more than evident that citizens are withdrawing and disengaging from the arena of conventional politics. Even when they vote, and this is less often than before, or in smaller proportions, their preferences emerge closer and closer to the moment of voting itself, and are now less easily guided by cohesive partisan cues. For whatever reason, and there is no shortage of hypotheses offering to explain this change, there are now fewer and fewer standpatters, and hence more and more citizens who, when they think about politics at all, are likely to operate on the basis of short-term considerations and influences. Electorates in this sense are becoming progressively destructured, affording more scope to the media to play the role of agenda-setter, and requiring a much greater campaign effort from parties and candidates. What we see here, in short, is a form of voting behaviour that is increasingly contingent, and a type of voter whose choices appear increasingly accidental or even random. Much of this change has only become really apparent since the end of the 1980s.

To be sure, we are dealing with sometimes quite small pieces of evidence here, and the changes which have been noted are also sometimes, though not always, relatively marginal – a trickle rather than a flood. But it is also important to appreciate that when all these disparate pieces of evidence, great and small, are summed together, they offer a very clear indication of a marked shift in the prevailing patterns of mass politics. This shift is not only consistent in focus – that is, all of these indicators now point in a common direction – but is also remarkably consistent across the range of polities. The conclusion is then clear: all over western Europe, and in all likelihood all over the advanced democracies, citizens are heading for the exits of the national political arena.

In early 2002, in an interview with the Dutch social science magazine *Facta*, Anthony Giddens drew attention to the changes that were being wrought in mass media entertainment through the growing popularity of docu-soaps and reality television. 'A watershed has been passed here,' he noted. 'Previously television was something that reflected an external world which people then watched. Now television is much more a medium in which you can participate.[8] In conventional politics, by contrast, the shift has been the other way around. Previously, and probably through to at least the 1970s, conventional politics was seen to belong to the citizen, to be something in which the citizen could easily participate, and often did participate. Now, to paraphrase Giddens, conventional politics has become part of an external world which people view from outside. There is a world of the parties, or a world of political leaders, that is separate from the world of the citizenry. As Bernard Manin (1997: 218–35) put it, we are witnessing

---

8. Interview with Anthony Giddens by Henk Jansen in *Facta*, 11:1, February 2003, 2–5, at 4 (my translation).

the transformation of party democracy into 'audience democracy'.[9] Whether the increasing withdrawal and disengagement of voters is responsible for the emergence of this new mode of democratic politics, or whether it is an emerging form of democratic politics that is encouraging voter withdrawal and disengagement is, at least for now, a moot point. What is beyond dispute is that each feeds the other. As citizens exit the national political arena, they inevitably weaken the major actors who survive there – the political parties. And this, in turn, is part of, and promotes, audience democracy. As Giovanni Sartori (2002: 78) puts it, 'video politics' – and hence also audience democracy – is stronger when parties are weak, and weaker when parties are strong. Strong parties are difficult to sustain when politics turns into a spectator sport, and that it should turn into a spectator sport is hardly surprising given the fading of the real differences that divided the parties in the first place. When mainstream party competition matters little for the substance of decision-making, it is only to be expected that it should drift towards an emphasis on theatre and spectacle.

---

9. For a comparable discussion, see Statera (1986), and especially Sartori (2002). For an earlier version of some of the arguments here, see Mair (1998).

2

THE CHALLENGE TO PARTY GOVERNMENT

The conflicts that divide political parties in the older democracies of western Europe have attenuated substantially in the past thirty years. This has occurred at two different levels. In the first place, there has been a reduction in the intensity of ideological polarization, as formerly 'anti-system' parties – that is, parties that challenge the fundamental principles on which democratic regimes are founded, and espouse a wholly alternative political settlement – have either moderated their demands and thus moved closer to the mainstream, or experienced significant losses in their electoral support. On the right, for example, the former anti-system alternative has now all but disappeared, and been replaced by far-right or national populist parties, which, though often espousing very radical and anti-consensual policy positions, do not claim to challenge the democratic regime as such (Mudde, 2007). Indeed, in more recent years, it has often proved quite easy for mainstream parties of the centre right to incorporate such parties into government – whether as fully fledged coalition partners, as in the case of the Austrian Freedom Party, for example, the Italian National Alliance or the Dutch Pim Fortuyn List; or as formal support parties for minority governments, as in the case of the Danish People's Party.

Anti-system parties of the left have also tended to moderate or fade away. In the wake of the collapse of the Soviet Union, for example, communist parties either gave up the ghost or transformed themselves into more widely acceptable social-democratic alternatives, and those that chose the latter route have also enjoyed access to government office. Even Sinn Féin, once the political wing of what was a very active and highly visible terrorist group, the IRA, now shares power in the devolved government of Northern Ireland. Green parties, for their part, quickly abandoned their pretensions to operate outside the system and were easily incorporated in broad-based centre-left coalitions. In a way that would have been unthinkable in the 1950s and 1960s, therefore, more or less all west European parties have now entered the political mainstream and become *salonfähig*. In electoral politics, only the democratic alternative is now on offer.[1]

Although this new form of consensus may now be taken for granted, it represents quite a fundamental shift from the patterns that prevailed even as late as the 1970s. Consider the situation in Italy, for example, where the contrast can be most visibly marked. In the mid-1970s, the key dynamic in Italian politics was that associated with the so-called 'historic compromise', by which the powerful Italian Communist party (PCI), then the strongest such party in western Europe, had come to knock on the door of cabinet office. The issue

---

1. For a number of recent evaluations and analyses of these processes in the pages of *West European Politics*, see Downs (2001); Heinisch (2003); Minkenberg (2001); van Spanje and van der Brug (2007).

of communist participation had come to a head in January 1978, with the resignation of Giulio Andreotti's minority Christian Democrat (DC) government – the thirty-fifth DC-led government since 1946, and the most recent in a long row of unstable ruling combinations all based on the exclusion of the PCI on the left and the small neo-fascist Italian Social Movement (MSI) on the right. By early 1978, however, it appeared impossible to reconstitute such a government again, leaving the only remaining option that of formally incorporating the PCI into the parliamentary majority. For many commentators, both inside and outside Italy, this was an extremely worrying prospect. So much so, indeed, that it prompted an exceptional public warning from the US State Department, which on 12 January 1978, midway through the one-term presidency of the Democrat Jimmy Carter, issued the following statement:

> Our position is clear: we do not favor [Communist participation in Western governments] and would like to see Communist influence in any Western European country reduced ... The United States and Italy share profound democratic values and interests, and we do not believe that the Communists share those values and interests. As the President [Carter] said in Paris last week: 'It is precisely when democracy is up against difficult challenges that its leaders must show firmness in resisting the temptation of finding solutions in non-democratic forces.'[2]

The same argument was echoed by the former US secretary of state Henry Kissinger in a review of the electoral successes and potential successes of communist parties in Italy, France, Portugal and Spain. For Kissinger (Ranney 1978: 184–85), 'the accession to power of Communists in an allied country would represent a massive change in European politics; ... would have fundamental

---

2. Quoted in Ranney (1978: 1).

consequences for the structure of the postwar world as we have known it and for America's relationship to its most important alliances; and … would alter the prospects for security and progress for all free nations.' At a time of renewed cold war, in other words, the communist electoral alternative was simply unacceptable. The ideological gap was too wide, and the strategic intentions as well as the legitimacy of the party itself were too deeply suspect.

In the event, of course, the PCI never did win admittance to government. Andreotti went on to form a new minority administration and continued his successful career in US-friendly politics until his party collapsed in a wave of corruption scandals and he himself was brought before the courts on charges of complicity in Mafia-related crimes. Indeed, it was not until 1996 that the more moderate successors to the PCI, the Party of the Democratic Left (PDS), finally entered government as the then leading party in a broad-based centre-left coalition, under the leadership of Romano Prodi, later president of the European Commission. Three years later, this government again came into close contact with a US administration, this time led by Bill Clinton, the first Democrat to hold the presidency since Carter. In November 1999, Clinton travelled to Florence to take part in an international gathering of various national political leaders. The purpose of the meeting was to discuss their shared styles of politics, with the intention of sketching out a blueprint for 'Progressive Governance for the 21st Century'. Among the other national leaders taking part in these 'Third Way' discussions were Fernando Henrique Cardoso from Brazil, Tony Blair from the UK, Lionel Jospin from France and Gerhard Schröder from Germany. More strikingly, the meeting itself was hosted and chaired by Massimo d'Alema, then leader of the PDS – that is, the former Communist party

– and by then also head of the new Italian centre-left government. Now that the Cold War was over, his party was no longer seen – by the Americans or by others – as a threat to the prospects of all free nations. On the contrary, it was now being heralded as a co-creator of the putative blueprint for progress. For d'Alema himself, meanwhile, 'the most "progressive" undertaking we [the Italian centre-left] have accomplished has been to get the national accounts in order and take the lira into the European currency by cutting inflation, lowering inter- est rates.'[3] This was a far cry from threatening the future of the free world.

While times have changed for parties trying to survive outside the mainstream, they have also changed for those inside the boundaries of conventional politics. This is the second level at which major changes can be highlighted. Just three years before Kissinger and the US State Department warned Italy about stretching its government too far, the noted political scientist S.E. Finer (1975) was mounting a major assault on what he called Britain's 'adversary politics'. Britain was then characterized by a highly competitive pattern of two- party politics. The Labour party had governed, at first with a tiny majority, then with a landslide, from 1964 to 1970, when it lost to the Conservatives, who held office with a modest majority until March 1974. Labour then returned as a minority government, and, follow- ing a second election in late 1974, managed to retain office with a small overall majority. The party remained in office until 1979, when it lost its working majority and was then displaced by Margaret Thatcher's first

3. The text of his contribution is reprinted in *Progressive Governance for the XXI Century: Conference Proceedings Florence, 20 and 21 November 1999*. Florence: European University Institute and New York University School of Law, 2000, 42.

Conservative government. From that point on, what had been a classic two-party system shifted towards what might better be seen as an alternating predominant party system, with the Conservatives holding power through three further elections, usually with massive majorities, followed by Labour with its own overwhelming majority in 1997, and the further victories of 2001 and 2005. In the mid-1970s, however, the pattern was obviously much more changeable, competitive and adversarial, and it was this that was of particular concern to Finer. Not only did the politics of the time reflect a marked degree of polarization and conflict; there was also a dramatic policy see-saw, with each newly incumbent government seeking to undo the policies that had been promoted by its predecessor. For Finer, British politics had deteriorated into 'a stand-up fight between two adversaries for the favour of the lookers-on ... [and] what sharpens this contestation is that the stakes are extremely high'. Later, in the same book, *Adversary Politics and Electoral Reform*, he spoke disparagingly of 'the discontinuities, the reversals, the extremisms of the existing system' (1975: 3, 32). A similar concern was voiced by the rather self-serving Lord Hailsham, a veteran of Conservative cabinets, who complained that the British system was becoming 'an elective dictatorship', in which the opposition was powerless in the face of strongly partisan government programmes.[4]

Since the last years of the Thatcher governments, however, and in sharp contrast to this earlier pattern, the parties in Britain have rushed to the centre, with the win-win politics of New Labour's 'Third Way' in particular being promoted as a way of superseding ideology and partisanship as central forces in the process

---

4. Hailsham's speech is reprinted in *The Listener*, 21 October 1976. After the 1979 election, Hailsham went on to become a leading member of the strongly partisan governments of Margaret Thatcher.

of policy-making. In place of the politics of party, and
hence in place of the reversals and extremisms of the
earlier system, there came what Burnham (1999, 2001)
has identified as 'the politics of depoliticization' – a
governing strategy in which decision-making authority is passed over to ostensibly non-partisan bodies and
in which binding rules are adopted which deny discretion to the government of the day. This was a politics
couched in strictly non-party terms, and in the British
case in particular it was presented as a new synthesis
overcoming the traditional divisions of left and right and
as such non-contestable: the politics of 'what works'.
As Britain's two-party system gave way to alternating
periods of predominance, so too adversarial politics
gave way to a new centrist consensus. The parties might
still compete with one another for votes, sometimes even
intensively, but they came to find themselves sharing the
same broad commitments in government and confin-
ing themselves to the same ever-narrowing repertoire of
policy-making.

The increased sharing of commitments is also evident
in other systems, and particularly those in which there is a
pronounced separation of powers, and/or those in which
government is usually formed by a coalition of parties.
In France, at least prior to the reform that shortened the
presidential term, it had become quite common to see
a form of US-style 'divided government,' whereby left-
wing presidents cohabited with right-wing parliaments
and governments, or vice versa, with both sides being
more or less obliged to find agreement, or consensus, on
what government did. Across the continental European
parliamentary systems, the basis for consensus and the
sharing of commitments has also become more marked.
In the Netherlands, for example, precedent was broken
when in 1994, for the first time in Dutch history, a new
government coalition was formed bringing together in

one cabinet the Labour party and the right-wing Liberal party, the two formations that, up to that point, had constituted the main alternative poles within the system. In Ireland, the traditional bipolar pattern of competition was irrevocably broken in 1993 when Labour, long the parliamentary ally of Fine Gael, crossed the traditional 'civil war' divide to form a government with Fianna Fáil. In Germany, a few years later, a new coalition brought the Greens and Social Democrats together in government, and, as a result of the institutional constraints that operate in the German Federal Republic, forced both to work together with the opposition Christian Democrats, the party that held sway in the powerful upper house of parliament. In contemporary politics, in other words, it has become less and less easy for any one party or bloc of parties to monopolize power, with the result that shared government has become more common.[5] As all parties become coalitionable, more or less, coalition-making has become more promiscuous. This, together with the need for balance across separated domestic and European institutions, has inevitably led policy-making to become less partisan.

DO PARTIES MATTER?

This last assertion is important and requires some justification. Since at least the late 1970s, a large number of political scientists from a variety of scholarly traditions have spent countless hours assessing, evaluating and debating research into the impact of parties on public policy, and discussing whether partisanship in government can be related to policy-making, policy choices and policy outputs (for early assessments, see Rose,

5. See also Laver and Shepsle (1991), who discuss this in the context of minority governments.

1980; Castles, 1982). Initially, the balance of the argument seemed to favour the relevance of partisanship – the 'parties-do-matter' school. The radical conservative governments led by Ronald Reagan and Margaret Thatcher, and the sudden shift towards a neo-liberal consensus in the 1980s, offered telling testimony in this regard, while over the course of the decades, a series of more or less sophisticated cross-national comparisons also emphasized the impact of parties, whether or not in conjunction with other socio-structural, institutional or political determinants of outcomes (see Schmidt, 1996; Keman, 2002). In sum, the evidence suggested that partisan differences mattered.

This view also persisted even into the 1990s, despite the expectation that any residual partisan effects might have been undermined by the growing impact of globalization. In a much-cited analysis that incorporated evidence up to the late 1980s, for example, Geoffrey Garrett argued that globalization had failed to erode either national autonomy (in the sense that it had not prevented nations forging their own policy solutions), or the capacity of left-wing or social-democratic governments to pursue policies aimed at reducing market-generated inequalities. In other words, despite globalization, countries and their governments – and hence also the parties in these governments – retained a major capacity for political control, suggesting that 'the impact of electoral politics has not been dwarfed by market dynamics' (1998: 2). Garrett went on to advance two main reasons for this conclusion. First, far from disempowering partisan constituencies, globalization had actually 'generated new political constituencies for left-of-centre parties among the increasing ranks of the economically insecure that offset the shrinking of the manufacturing working class'; second, globalization offered new 'political incentives for left-wing parties to pursue economic policies that redistribute wealth and risk in favour of those adversely affected in the short term by market dislocations' (1998: 10, 11). Even in the changed circumstances of late-twentieth-century politics, therefore, party differences and left-right oppositions still played a major role in the policy-making process.

However, while another highly authoritative analysis of the impact of partisan politics on macroeconomic policies (Boix, 1998) came to similar conclusions, in this case the most recent evidence appeared to suggest an actual weakening of the relationship over time. When first faced with pressure to liberalize financial markets in the 1980s, for example, non-socialist governments tended to act quite quickly, whereas socialist governments delayed or even resisted the process. By the end of the decade, however, these differences had evaporated, and 'an autonomous monetary policy became extremely hard to pursue' (Boix, 1998: 70). Indeed, Garrett's later figures were also beginning to tell a different story. Looking at data that stretched into the 1990s, and in contrast to his earlier conclusions, he now found there was much more support for the idea that globalization limited domestic autonomy and hence helped to force parties into common positions (Garrett, 2000: 36–37). This conclusion was echoed in other contemporaneous analyses of policy profiles and outcomes. Within the traditionally contentious area of welfare policy, for example, Evelyne Huber and John Stephens's exhaustive analysis showed ample evidence of the 'reduction and then the disappearance of partisan effects' (2001: 321), while Miki Caul and Mark Gray's analysis of party manifesto data showed a strong tendency to convergence between left and right, such that already by the end of the 1980s, 'political parties across advanced industrial democracies increasingly find it difficult to maintain distinct identities' (2000: 235).

In itself, this slide into declining partisanship is hardly surprising. Parties were always more likely to matter in the so-called Golden Age of embedded liberalism, from the 1950s to the early 1970s, when they were relatively unconstrained in shaping the policy outcomes that might matter to their electorates. As Fritz Scharpf (2000: 24; see also Ruggie, 1982) has put it, national governments and the parties that formed them could then easily shelter behind 'semi-permeable economic boundaries ... [and] ignore the exit options of capital owners, tax payers and consumers.' By the late 1970s and early 1980s, however, the domestic capacity to control the economic environment was already in decline, with the end of the Golden Age signalled by the breakdown of the Bretton Woods system of fixed exchange rates and the first major oil-price crisis. By then, as Scharpf (2000: 27–29) goes on to point out, governments were losing not only their ability to shape the economy but also their desire to do so, and it was this shift in orientation as much as circumstance that was later to create the widespread waves of deregulation, privatization, and liberalization. Ruggie (1997: 7) had come to similar conclusions, arguing in his reflections on the end of embedded liberalism that the expansion and integration of global capital markets in the 1990s had 'eroded traditional instruments of economic policy while creating wholly new policy challenges that neither governments nor market players yet fully understand let alone can fully manage'.

But it is not just the *supply* of partisan policy-making that determines whether parties make a difference; it is also a matter of what is *demanded* at the electoral level. Manfred Schmidt (2002: 168) has usefully pointed out that the very logic of the 'parties-matter' thesis builds from two core propositions: first, that the 'social constituencies of political parties in constitutional democracies have *distinctive preferences* and successfully feed the process of policy formation with these preferences'; and second, that the 'policy orientations of political parties broadly *mirror* the preferences of their *social constituencies*' (see also Keman, 2002). It follows that in the absence of such constituencies there is little by way of collective preferences that can be mirrored, even if the parties could or wished to mirror them, and hence the whole logic of the partyness of policy-making becomes difficult to sustain.

DECLINING ELECTORAL COHESION

It is beyond dispute that the once-distinct electorates of the mainstream political parties in western Europe have become markedly less cohesive in the past two to three decades. To be sure, it can be shown that traditional cleavages remain relevant to voting behaviour. For all the changes that have been wrought in the economy and in the polity over the past decades, for example, workers are still more likely than the middle class to vote for left-of-centre parties, and active church attenders are still more likely than secular voters to support religious parties. This is undeniable (e.g., Elff, 2007). But what is also clear is that the relative weight of these voting determinants has declined. Church attenders might still vote along religious lines, but there are many fewer such citizens in European electorates than there were thirty years ago, and their capacity to shape electoral politics has diminished accordingly (Best, 2011). The shifts in class voting are even more marked. The core working-class constituencies have experienced pronounced demographic decline, while the homogeneity of political preferences within the remaining class cohorts has been lost. In the most comprehensive and nuanced comparative study to date, Oddbjørn Knutsen (2006) points to a substantial decline, both absolute and relative, in class voting in western Europe since the mid-1970s, with the falls being most pronounced in precisely those polities where class had once been a very strong predictor of political preference (see also Knutsen, 2007).

It is also beyond dispute that, in responding to, and sometimes even provoking, the changes in their electoral alignments, parties have become electorally more catch-all, easing their grip on once-core social constituencies while extending their appeal ever more broadly across traditional class and religious lines. In part, of course, this is the inevitable result of social change. Since the core constituencies themselves have begun to decline or to fragment, there is less within the social structure for the parties to grip on to (see also Freire, 2006). Voters have become more 'particularized' (Franklin et al., 1992). But in coming to terms with this social change, the individual parties have also had to learn to be more attractive to those segments of the electorate once seen as beyond the pale: religious parties have had to learn to appeal to secular voters, socialist parties to middle-class voters, liberal parties to working-class voters, and farmers parties to urban voters. In other words, it is not only that the vote has become more free-floating and available: so also have the parties themselves, with the result that political competition has come to be characterized by the contestation of socially inclusive appeals in search of support from socially amorphous electorates.

The tendency towards the decline of collective identities within western electorates, resulting from more or less common socio-economic or socio-cultural processes, has therefore been further accentuated at the political level by the behaviour and strategies of the competing political parties, and one consequence of this has been to undermine the foundations of partisanship in policy-making and in government. Given the

absence of coherent and relatively enduring social constituencies, there is little remaining on which parties can
build or identify stable alignments. To be sure, ad hoc
constituencies of the kind inevitably constructed in the
process of electoral campaigning may also be marked
by distinct sets of preferences, and such sets of preferences may be more or less sharply in competition with
one another; but these are hardly likely to match the
enduring identities and interests that characterized the
traditional core constituencies of cleavage politics, and
are therefore unlikely to be understood – or assumed –
with the same degree of conviction by political leaders.
It is in this sense that catch-allism in politics, like the
social conditions that foster it, drives out partisanship.

In fact, as was shown in the previous chapter, the
decline of partisan identities is one of the most telling
changes in European mass politics in the last thirty
years. Russell Dalton (2004: 32), who has documented
this in some detail and with unambiguous results, suggests that 'if party attachments reflect citizen support for
the system of party-based representative government,
then the simultaneous decline in party attachments ...
offers a strong sign of the public's affective disengagement from political authorities.' Voters might still line
up behind one or other of the competing parties at election time – as yet, there obviously remains no case of a
single party winning 100 per cent of the vote in open
competition, or of a total set of parties failing to register
even 1 per cent of the poll – but who these voters are,
or for how long they will remain aligned, becomes less
and less predictable. There is greater uncertainty about
whether any individual citizen will go to the polls, and,
even if she votes, there is greater uncertainty about the
preference she might reveal. In this sense, voting patterns have become less structured, more random, and
hence also increasingly unpredictable and inconsistent.

In France in 2007, for example, in the space of a brief eight-week period, there occurred a presidential election that registered a record high turnout of 84 per cent, and a legislative election that registered a record low turnout of 60 per cent (Sauger, 2007).

Let me try to draw these strands together. In many different respects – including their patterns of incumbency, their policy commitments, and their electoral profiles – parties within the mainstream have become less easily distinguished from one another than they were in the polities of the late 1970s. Despite the growing evidence of bipolar competition (see below), the parties now share government with one another more easily and more readily, with any lingering differences in policy-seeking goals appearing to matter less than the shared cross-party ambition for office. Policy discretion has become increasingly constrained by the imperatives of globalization, and, within the much-expanded European Union and and European Free Trade Association area, by the disciplines imposed by the Growth and Stability Pact and the European Central Bank. Even when parties are in government, in other words, the freedom for partisan manoeuvre is severely limited, and this too makes the task of differentiating between parties or between governments more difficult. Finally, a combination of increasing social homogenization – the blurring of traditional identity boundaries – and increasing individualization has cut across differences in partisan electoral profiles, leaving most of the mainstream protagonists chasing more or less the same bodies of voters with more or less the same suasive techniques. Through the sharing of office, programmes and voters, even as competing coalitions, the parties have become markedly less distinct from one another, while partisan purpose is itself seen as less meaningful or even desirable.

THE PROBLEM OF PARTY GOVERNMENT

This also serves to undermine the notion of party government. Party government is a rather elusive concept that did not begin to receive attention in European political science until the late 1960s. By then, however, it was already a prominent theme in discussions of US politics, with the American Political Science Association's 1950 report, *Towards a More Responsible Two-Party System*, at the centre of debates over political and institutional reform. This much-cited and later much-criticized report had been heavily influenced by the work of E.E. Schattschneider, who emphasized the need for effective choice and accountability in federal elections. As he argued in 1945: 'The major party in a two-party system is typically and essentially a mobilizer of majorities for the purpose of taking control of the government; it is the most potent form of democratic political organization available for our use. The major party is the only political organization in American public life which is in a position to make a claim, upon any reasonable grounds whatsoever, that it can measure up to the requirements of modern public policy... It alone submits its claims to the nation in a general election in which the stakes are a mandate from the people to govern the country' (Schattschneider, 1945: 1151). In US practice, however, these arguments fall rather flat, with many of the early responses to the APSA report suggesting that it was oriented towards a British-style of cabinet government and majoritarian democracy, a system that was anathema to many American observers (see Kirkpatrick, 1971). Nor did the arguments receive much support in Europe. In this case, it was again a British or perhaps Anglo-American two-party model that seemed to be favoured, with the result that the arguments themselves appeared largely irrelevant (see Daalder, 1987).

The first substantial attempt to address the issue of party government in the European context was developed by Richard Rose (1969) and was also heavily biased towards the Anglo-American experience, although the analysis itself concluded with an attempt to draw more wide-ranging cross-national conclusions and to elaborate a series of hypotheses that could be tested in a wide variety of systems.[6] For Rose, party government is about the capacity of parties to 'translate possession of the highest formal offices of a regime into operational control of government' (1969: 413). And since this capacity varied from system to system, and also over time, his analysis sought to identify the more specific conditions that must be met for parties to influence government. These are listed in Box 1, overleaf, and may be summarized as requiring a winning party to have identifiable policies and the organizational and institutional capacity to carry them out through the people it appoints for that purpose. It is this that constitutes 'operational control of government' and hence what may be defined in these circumstances as the practice of 'party government'. In the absence of these conditions, alternative forms of government may be identified, among which Rose lists government by charismatic leadership, traditional government, military government, government 'by inertia', and in particular 'administrative government', whereby 'civil servants not only maintain routine services of government, but also try to formulate new policies' (1969: 418).

A similar but more parsimonious list of conditions for party government was later elaborated by Richard Katz (1986: 43–44) in a more abstract analysis that

6. Rose's 1969 article was later reprinted in his *The Problem of Party Government* (Rose, 1974), which as a whole, despite its title, goes no further in dealing with party government as such than did the original article.

Box 1. *Rose: conditions for party government*

1. At least one party must exist and, after some form of contest, it must become dominant in the regime.
2. Nominees of the party then occupy important positions in the regime.
3. The number of partisans nominated for office is large enough to permit partisans to participate in the making of a wide range of policies.
4. The partisans in office must have the skills necessary to control large bureaucratic organizations.
5. Partisans must formulate policy intentions for enactment once in office.
6. Policy intentions must be stated in a 'not unworkable' form.
7. Partisans in office must give high priority to carrying out party policies.
8. The party policies that are promulgated must be put into practice by the personnel of the regime.

Source: Rose (1969: 416–18)

---

was intended for application to a wide variety of parliamentary and presidential systems. For Katz, party government required three conditions. First, all major governmental decisions were to be taken by people chosen in electoral contests conducted along party lines, or at least by individuals appointed by and responsible to such people. Second, policy was to be decided within the governing party or by negotiations among parties in the case of coalition governments. In this sense policy was to be made on party lines 'so that each party may be collectively accountable for "its" position' (1986: 43). Third, the highest officials (ministers, prime ministers) were to be selected within parties and to be held responsible for their actions and policies through parties. Most important, this third condition implied that 'positions in government must flow from support within the party rather than party positions flowing from electoral success' (1986: 43). In a later study, Katz (1987: 7) adapted these conditions into the five interrelated stipulations shown in Box 2. That is, party government is manifest when winning parties both decide and enact policies through officials who are recruited and held accountable by parties. Katz also follows Rose (1969) in identifying a series of alternatives to party government,

---

Box 2. *Katz: conditions for party government*

1. Decisions are made by elected party officials or by those under their control.
2a. Policy is decided within parties which
2b. then act cohesively to enact it.
3a. Officials are recruited and
3b. held accountable through parties.

Source: Katz (1987: 7)

---

derived in this case from the concrete analyses developing from his model: corporatist or neo-corporatist government, in which policies are set through negotiations between interests that are directly affected by the policies; pluralist democracy, in which each individual candidate and elected official is responsible to his or her own constituency, and in which party as such does not figure; and direct democracy, in which policies are determined by referendum and elections are not decisive for securing mandates or accountability (Katz, 1987: 18–20).[7]

The decisiveness of the electoral process and a strong foundation of electoral accountability are also central in a later version of the party government model elaborated by Jacques Thomassen (1994). In this case the emphasis is less on party government as such, and more on the role of elections as a mechanism of linkage and

---

7. Laver and Shepsle (1994: 5–8) also briefly list a variety of alternatives to party government, including bureaucratic, legislative, prime-ministerial, cabinet and ministerial forms. See also Müller (1994).

representation. Nevertheless, though differently oriented, the core conditions of Thomassen's party government model and, as he emphasizes, of the 'responsible parties model', are quite similar to those of Rose and Katz (see Box 3) and are manifest when the will of the majority of the electorate is reflected in government policy.

Box 3. *Thomassen: conditions for party government*

1. Voters have a choice, in the sense that they can choose between at least two parties with different policy proposals.
2. The parties are sufficiently cohesive or disciplined to enable them to implement their policy.
3. Voters vote according to their policy preferences, that is, they choose the party that represents their policy preferences best. This is turn requires that:
   (a) voters have policy preferences, and
   (b) voters are aware of the differences between the programmes of different political parties.
4. The party or coalition winning the elections takes control of government.
5. Both the policy programmes of political parties and the policy preferences of voters are constrained by a single ideological dimension.

Source: Thomassen (1994)

These three sets of stipulations share much common ground, although the emphasis varies from policy-making in the case of Rose, to recruitment in the case of Katz, and the electoral connection in the case of Thomassen. If we try to synthesize them, bringing all three emphases together, then a single set of core stipulations can be suggested. Party government in democratic polities will prevail when a party or party bloc wins control of the executive as a result of competitive elections, when the political leaders in the polity are recruited by and through parties, when the (main) parties or alternatives in competition offer voters clear policy alternatives, when public policy is determined by the party or parties holding executive office and when that executive is held accountable through parties. These stipulations are summarized in Box 4. Equally, party government will not

---

Box 4. *Summary conditions for party government*

1. A party (parties) wins control of the executive as a result of competitive elections
2. Political leaders are recruited by and through parties
3. Parties offer voters clear policy alternatives
4. Public policy is determined by the party (parties) in the executive
5. The executive is held accountable through parties

---

prevail, or will certainly be severely weakened, should one or more of these conditions be absent.

My contention is that, as a result of long-term shifts in the character of elections, parties and party competition, it is precisely this set of conditions that is being undermined.[8]

THE WANING OF PARTY GOVERNMENT

It is impossible here to offer a full account of the changing conditions of party government.[9] What can be done, however, is to identify a series of key changes that bear on some of the conditions listed above, and together point towards a major shift in modes of government in contemporary Europe.

---

8. For an earlier evaluation of these problems, see Smith (1986).

9. For a different approach to the issue of party government, focusing more attention on the link between parties and the governing institutions, see Blondel and Cotta (2000). In this chapter, I focus mainly on the question of the power that may or may not travel from party to government. In the wider discussion of the cartel party (e.g. Katz and Mair, 1995; Katz and Mair, 2002), there is also a treatment of power that travels from government to party, and particularly to the party in public office.

I will begin with the condition that remains secure, and which, if anything, has become even more salient: that by which a party or parties win control of the executive as a result of competitive elections. This has always been the case in two-party systems, in which elections are decisive and the winning party at the polls goes on to form the government. These are also responsive systems, with wholesale alternation in government being both a normal expectation and a relatively frequent occurrence. There are other systems, however, where the condition might seem less likely to obtain, and these include in particular the more traditional 'continental' European systems, in which fragmented party groupings compete against one another in shifting multi-party coalitions, and a clear boundary between government and opposition has often proved difficult to identify. Wholesale alternation in these latter systems has also been a relatively rare occurrence, at least traditionally, since coalitions would usually overlap with one another, blurring the lines of overall responsibility and accountability as a result.

Over time, the balance of the European polities has appeared to shift in favour of the bipolar mode. This substantial change in the functioning of European party systems has come about in two ways (Bale, 2003; Mair, 2008). In the first place, bipolarity has become the norm in the new democracies in southern Europe, with what are effectively two-party systems emerging and consolidating in Greece, Portugal and Spain, as well as Malta. Second, bipolar competition is now also increasingly characteristic of many of the older multi-party systems. That is, even in those systems that are marked by quite pronounced party fragmentation, political competition is now more likely to mimic the two-party pattern through the creation of rival pre-electoral coalitions tending to divide voters into two contingent political camps. During the 1950s and 1960s, for example, the majority of European polities changed governments by means of shifting and overlapping centrist coalitions and rarely if ever offered voters a choice of alternative governments. During the 1990s, by contrast, almost two-thirds of these older polities experienced at least some two-party or two-bloc competition, usually involving wholesale alternation in government. To these two sets of changes may also be added a third, this time in a context of largely unstructured party systems, in that a number of the post-communist polities have also drifted towards more bipolar competition. In sum, if party government depends on electoral contests that can produce a clear distinction between winners and losers, then this condition was being met more frequently at the close of the twentieth century than was ever the case in the early postwar decades.

The other conditions listed in Box 4 have proved much less robust, however. Although political leaders continue to be recruited by party, for example, they are less likely to be recruited *through* parties, in that the choice of leader is now less often determined by the strength of a candidate's support within the party and more often by the candidate's capacity to appeal to the media and thence to the wider electorate. The choice of Blair rather than Brown in the leadership contest in the British Labour party offered a clear example of this shift, as did the preference for Schröder over Lafontaine in the near-contemporaneous debate over who was to be the SPD's candidate for the chancellorship of Germany.[10]

---

10. The version of the German story as told by a clearly peevish Oskar Lafontaine (2000: 50–57) carries extraordinarily strong echoes of the version of the British story that was reported by various allies of Gordon Brown to Andrew Rawnsley (2000). As Lafontaine puts it, having admitted that Schröder cut the better figure on television: 'Is it permissible ... for the media to have the decisive voice in a discussion over who shall lead a party into an election campaign? If the party were

Such passages, combined with the clear evidence of the 'presidentialization' of political leadership in parliamentary democracies (Poguntke and Webb, 2005), suggest the formation of a more direct kind of linkage between political leaders and the electorate, one less strongly mediated by political parties as organizations.

Moreover, as suggested above, the parties are also less able – and perhaps less willing – to offer clear policy alternatives to voters. Whether circumscribed by global and European constraints, or whether limited by the inability to identify any clear constituency within the electorate that is sufficiently large and cohesive to offer a mandate for action, parties increasingly tend to echo one another and to blur what might otherwise be clear policy choices. To be sure, there is a choice between the competing teams of leaders, and given the growing evidence of bipolarity, that particular choice is becoming more sharply defined. But there is less and less choice in policy terms, suggesting that political competition is drifting towards an opposition of form rather than of content. Competition in these circumstances can be intense and hard-fought, but it is often akin to the competition on show in football matches or horse races: sharp, exciting and even pleasing to the spectators, but ultimately lacking in substantive meaning. It was precisely this that Kirchheimer (1957) long ago associated with the 'elimination' of opposition – the situation that prevails when polities experience government by cartel, and when no meaningful differences divide protagonists, however vigorously they may at times compete with one another.

Likewise, public policy is no longer so often decided by the party, or even under its direct control. Instead, with the rise of the regulatory state, decisions are increasingly

---

to answer this question in the affirmative, would it not be shedding too much of its own responsibility?' (2000: 52).

passed to non-partisan bodies that operate at arms length from party leaders – the 'non-majoritarian' or 'guardian' institutions (Majone, 1994). Faced with increasing environmental constraints, as well as with the growing complexity of legislation and policy-making in a transnational context, there is inevitably a greater resort to delegation and depoliticization (Thatcher and Stone Sweet, 2003). Moreover, the officials who work within these delegated bodies are less often recruited directly through the party organization,[11] and are increasingly held accountable by means of judicial and regulatory controls. And since this broad network of agencies forms an ever larger part of a dispersed and pluriform executive, operating both nationally and supranationally, the very notion of accountability being exercised through parties, or of the executive being held answerable to *voters* (as distinct from citizens or stakeholders) becomes problematic. Party, in this sense, loses much of its representative and purposive identity, and in this way citizens forfeit much of their capacity to control policymakers through conventional electoral channels.

Above all, it is here that we see the conditions for the maintenance of party government being undermined, and where the alternative forms of government identified by Rose (1969) begin to acquire greater historical weight, notably both government by inertia and 'administrative government'. This is the sort of shift identified also by Johannes Lindvall and Bo Rothstein (2006: 61) in their analysis of the decline of the 'strong state' model in Sweden: 'the state ... is no longer an instrument for the political parties that dominate the Riksdag to steer and change society. Instead, the administrative state is turning into another ideological battlefield, where

---

11. Although they may well be controlled by an autonomous political leadership, suggesting a 'party as network' notion that seems markedly different from the more traditional forms of party organization.

sectoral interests seek power and influence ... [and in which] the role of political parties as the main producers of policy-oriented ideology and ideas is challenged.'

There is one other respect in which the conditions for the maintenance of party government are severely undermined, but in this case one that has received relatively scant attention. In Thomassen's account, summarized above in Box 3, a key condition for party government and for the responsible parties model is that both the policy programmes of the parties and the policy preferences of the voters be inscribed in, and constrained by, a single ideological dimension. The reasoning behind this argument is straightforward. Should two or more dimensions be invoked as the plane of contestation, it would be impossible for either the voters or the parties to establish a relationship based on representation and accountability, since it would never be clear precisely which positions on which dimension had favoured support for one particular alternative over another. In other words, the requirement of popular control that is included in the various sets of conditions given by the other authors (1, 5 and 6 in Rose's set; 1 and 3b in Katz's; 1, 3 and 5 in the summary set) calls for a shared recognition by voters and parties of the policy choices that are on offer and of the commitment to implement these policies, and also, it follows, for the sort of clarity that is intrinsically unavailable in a multi-dimensional space (Thomassen 1994: 252–57 and fn. 3). Moreover, as Thomassen goes on to suggest, and as is clear from the work of Sani and Sartori (1983) among others, the only possible single dimension that can meet this requirement is that of left-right opposition, which alone is sufficiently elastic and pervasive to accommodate the various domains of voter identification, and at the same time sufficiently enduring to provide a stable reference point over time. It is difficult to imagine any other dimension that might offer the same degree of coherence and clarity to the electorate and the parties taken as a whole. In the absence of a left-right plane of competition, in other words, the entire foundation of the party government/responsible parties model is undermined.

It is here that the challenge to party government may be most sharply defined. Briefly put, and building on a variety of different arguments, it may be argued that the left-right divide, even in its simplest form, is now finally losing coherence (Mair, 2007). Voters in contemporary Europe may still be willing to locate themselves in left-right terms, and may even be willing to locate the parties in the same dimension, but the meanings associated with these distinctions are becoming increasingly diverse and confused. In part, this is due to the policy convergence between parties; in part also, to the often contradictory signals emerging from post-communist Europe, whereby the traditional left position is often seen as the most conservative. In another respect, it has to do with the new challenge of liberalism, and the increasingly heterogeneous coalition that has begun to define leftness in anti-imperial or anti-American terms, bringing together former communists, religious fundamentalists and critical social movements within what may appear to be a unified ideological camp. In this context, meanings are no longer shared and the implications of political stances on the left or on the right become almost unreadable.

This is the essence of the argument developed by Russell Hardin (2000) in an important essay on the problems of understanding political trust and distrust. Hardin argues that there have been two important changes in the way political issues have come to be understood and treated in contemporary democracies. The first is 'the essential end, at least for the near term, of the focus on economic distribution and the management of the economy for production and distribution' (Hardin, 2000: 41–42).

In other words, echoing Scharpf's and Ruggie's obser-
vations on the end of embedded liberalism, he suggests
that governments are no longer capable of purposefully
managing the economy with a view to redistributing
resources or responding to collective needs, and that this
failing capacity has fundamentally altered traditional
political discourse. The issue of planning versus markets
has been settled – for now – in favour of the markets
(2000: 32), leaving much of the matter of conventional
political debate without a supporting context. The second
change is that problem-solving and decision-making in
public policy have become substantially more complex,
and hence less amenable to popular understanding or
control. Voters can no longer easily grasp the issues that
are at stake, and find it difficult to evaluate the often
quite technical alternatives that are presented to them.
The result of both changes, claims Hardin (2000: 42),
is to 'preclude the organization of politics along a single
left-right economic dimension', leading to a situation in
which the concerns of citizens become 'a hotchpotch of
unrelated issues that are not the obvious domain of any
traditional political party'. The left-right divide loses
its interpretive power as a schema for making overall
sense of mainstream politics, and is not replaced by any
alternative overarching paradigm. Demands become
particularized and fragmented, while party policy and
voter preferences evidence a lack of internal constraint
or cohesion. In these circumstances, it is almost impossible to imagine party government functioning effectively
or maintaining full legitimacy. Almost thirty years ago,
in the anniversary issue of *Daedalus*, Suzanne Berger
(1979: 30) argued that 'the critical issue for Western
Europe today is the capacity of the principal agencies of
political life – party, interest group, bureaucracy, legisla-
ture – to manage the problems of society and economy,
and, beyond coping, to redefine and rediscover common

purposes.' Today, it is their basic legitimacy as political institutions that is in doubt. Parties, like the other traditional agencies of the European polities, might well be accepted by citizens as necessary for the good functioning of politics and the state, but they are neither liked nor trusted, and one way in which we might better understand this change in perspective is by recognizing that although the trappings of party government may persist, the conditions for its maintenance as a functioning governmental mode are now at serious risk.

3

THE WITHDRAWAL OF THE ELITES

On the face of it, we might expect that the popular withdrawal from conventional politics discussed in Chapter 1 would leave a lot of angry and frustrated politicians in its wake. Indeed, given how difficult it is becoming to engage citizens in the conventional political arena, we might well expect that party and political leaders would devote considerable effort to trying to keep politics alive and meaningful, even if only in theatrical terms. And, at a certain level, this has been happening. Rarely has there been such widespread discussion of institutional reform, be it of the electoral system, parliamentary procedures, local or regional government, plebiscitary mechanisms or whatever. Almost none of the European democracies has been untouched by these discussions, and almost all have devoted considerable research effort to discussing the limitations of their present institutional arrangements and the ways in which they might be changed – sometimes quite drastically. Moreover, the single thread that runs through almost all of these discussions in almost all of the countries concerned is that reform is needed in order to bring government closer to the citizen. As Kaare Strøm and his colleagues conclude at the end of their long and exhaustive study of delegation and accountability in contemporary democracies, 'there is every reason to mind the gap between citizens and their political representatives.'[1] It was also what David Cameron, leader of the then opposition Conservatives, concluded in the wake of the MPs' expenses scandal that captured the headlines in Britain in early 2009: 'I believe the central objective of the new politics we need should be a massive, sweeping, radical redistribution of power. From the state to citizens; from the government to parliament; from Whitehall to communities. From the EU to Britain; from judges to the people; from bureaucracy to democracy. Through decentralisation, transparency and accountability we must take power away from the political elite and hand it to the man and woman in the street.'[2] It is in this sense that citizen discontent and disenchantment appear to prompt the elite to seek solutions through institutional change, as well as provoking quite pervasive official concern with how this ebbing of commitment might finally be stemmed.

That, at least, is how it appears on the surface. But along with the beating of official breasts and the show of distress at the hollowing out of mass politics, there exists in the practice of organized democracy a clear tendency to match citizen withdrawal with elite withdrawal. That is, just as citizens retreat to their own private and particularized spheres of interest, so too the political and party leaders retreat into their own version of this private and particular sphere, which is constituted by the closed world of the governing institutions.

---

1. See Strøm, Müller and Bergman (2003: 746).
2. 'David Cameron: I Would Reduce No 10's Power', *Guardian*, 26 May 2009, guardian.co.uk.

Disengagement is mutual, and for all the rhetoric that echoes on all sides, it is general.

THE CENTURY OF MASS POLITICS

In politics, just as in communications, culture and war, the twentieth century was the mass century. It is now more or less one hundred years since the last of the property qualifications that once limited the right to electoral participation began to be waived, such that in most west European democracies by the early 1900s elections were already, or soon would be, organized around the principle of mass democracy.[3] With mass democracy came the emergence of mass political parties. In some cases, the organization of these parties proceeded as a consequence of the democratization of elections – new waves of voters became available, and political parties, both old and new, sought to incorporate these new voters through the development of mass-membership organizations. In other cases, the mass parties had already been established, and it was often because of their pressure and insistence that the electoral arena had been expanded. Whatever the particular sequence, however, the coincidence was evident: mass democracies became associated with mass parties, which now became the defining party model for the new political age. Moreover, with the initial development of the mass party, political parties as such entered their golden age, an age in which, at least for a time, they dominated politics, constituting its principal point of reference.

---

3. It was, of course, initially a principle of mass male democracy, since voting rights for women were not usually granted until after World War I, and it was not until 1945 in France, 1948 in Belgium and as late as 1971 in Switzerland that women were allowed to participate and that universal and equal adult suffrage was finally achieved.

During this 'golden age', the mass parties in western Europe strove to establish more or less closed political communities, sustained by reasonably homogeneous electoral constituencies, strong and often hierarchical organizational structures and a coherent sense of partisan political identity. Voters, at least in the majority of cases, were believed to 'belong' to their parties, and rather than reflecting the outcome of a reasoned choice between the competing alternatives, the act of voting was seen instead as an expression of identity and commitment. As Richard Rose and Harve Mossawir (1967: 186) observed in an early review of voting studies, 'to speak of the majority of voters at a given election as "choosing" a party is nearly as misleading as speaking of a worshipper on a Sunday "choosing" to go to an Anglican, rather than a Presbyterian or Baptist church.' This was the politics of mass democracy as organized by mass parties, and one of the consequences of the rise of this party form was the relatively rapid stabilization or 'freezing' of collective political identities in the decades following the introduction of mass suffrage (Lipset and Rokkan, 1967).

In the main, these closed political communities were built on a foundation of closed social communities, in which large collectivities of citizens shared distinct social experiences, whether these were defined in terms of occupation, working and living conditions, religious practices, to name the most important. These social collectivities were in their turn cemented by the existence of vibrant and effective social institutions, including trade unions, churches, social clubs and so on. In other words, the closure of political communities usually derived from, or was based on, social closure, which, in a variety of European countries, tended to create a pattern of widespread segmentation, dividing social groups from one another while uniting their own individual 'members' and adherents. This is the process the Dutch have called 'pillarization', which was probably carried further in the Netherlands than in most other polities (see, for example, Lijphart, 1968; Houska, 1985). Viewing its operation elsewhere, we can see it as one in which political cleavage structures became consolidated (Bartolini and Mair, 1990: 212–49; Bartolini, 2000: 411–501).

At the same time, however, there was never any automatic or 'natural' translation of relevant social divisions into political oppositions and party formation. In and of themselves, for example, class structures largely failed to sustain a major socialist party in either the United States or Ireland, even though this development was the standardizing political experience in all other western democracies almost a century ago. Other social contrasts, and most notably gender, also failed in and of themselves to generate major political oppositions. Thus while social divisions helped to sustain political identities, they were not in themselves a sufficient precondition for the development of mass parties.

A second impetus was therefore usually required, and this came through the mass organizations themselves, and through the conscious intervention of party. In other words, by actively mobilizing citizens into a set of collective political identities, the political parties themselves helped to construct their own independent networks of partisan loyalties. Organizational intervention was crucial here, for in supplanting the loose-knit parties of notables that had flourished in the period prior to mass suffrage, the new parties approached their supporters with claims that, as Sigmund Neumann (1956: 404) put it, were 'incomparably greater' than those made by those earlier parties, in that they began to demand 'an increasing influence over all spheres of the individual's daily life'. And it was to be the interaction of both of these forces – social closure, on the one hand, and organizational intervention or encapsulation, on the other – that anchored the new mass parties and stabilized their support networks.

This, indeed, had always been the great strength of the classic west European mass parties in the early decades of the century, in that they managed to cement the loyalties of their voters by building strong organizational networks on the basis of shared social experiences. Organizational effort plus social closure spelt political identity and political endurance. In practice, of course, the strength of political identities varied both within and across countries, as did the relative balance between organizational effort and social closure. The British Labour party, for example, was built on the basis of a very powerful class identity, but always remained relatively weak in organizational terms, preferring to develop as a sort of federal party to which local organizations and trade unions could become affiliated. At the opposite extreme was the neighbouring Irish Fianna Fáil party, whose support patterns have always revealed few if any social correlates, but which built a strong and stable following on the basis of a strictly political appeal, on the one hand, and a powerful organizational network, on the other. The classic example of the combination of social closure and organizational effort was that of the Social Democrats in imperial Germany (Roth, 1963), who combined strong class support with a party network that genuinely attempted to forge 'cradle-to-grave' encapsulation. In France, by contrast, neither the social nor the organizational impetus proved particularly powerful, and the political parties that emerged, even on the left, tended to be more fissiparous and ephemeral.

Parties in this golden age were marked also by their mutual distinctiveness. Differences were conspicuous. As we have seen, each party had, or hoped to develop, its own 'natural' constituency within the wider society. Each had a distinct programme designed to reflect the interests of that constituency. Each sought to mobilize its own organizational resources, whether through its members or adherents, or through its own affiliated organizations, or through associated sponsors. Each maintained its own separate lines of communication, whether through a private party press or through the unequivocal partisan support of a national daily newspaper. Ideally, each hoped to form its own single-party government, or, should that prove impossible because of excessive fragmentation, to share government only with one or two like-minded competitors. In other words, and precisely because these parties maintained such distinct clienteles, representational integrity was a priority. They constituted the political voice of their constituencies, and derived both their strength and their legitimacy from that relationship.

The result was that European democracy became synonymous with party democracy, and European government with party government.[4] Within one agency or one institution, party guaranteed the two key constitutive elements of democracy: representation, on the one hand, and hence government *by* the people; and procedural legitimacy, on the other hand, or government *for* the people. In other words, parties – or at least the classic mass party – gave voice to the people, while also ensuring that the institutions of government were accountable. The party was at once representative *and* governor, and hence constituted, as Rudolf Wildenmann (1986) once put it, 'the crucial agency of institutional legitimation'.

* * *

---

4. See Francis G. Castles and Rudolf Wildenmann, eds., *Visions and Realities of Party Government*. Berlin: de Gruyter, 1986; and Jean Blondel and Maurizio Cotta (eds.), *The Nature of Party Government: A Comparative European Perspective*. Basingstoke: Palgrave, 2000.

The golden age of party has now passed, and one of the principal purposes of this book is to analyse some of the causes and implications of this great change of political condition. As for the passing itself, we can probably date the first major step in the process back to the middle 1960s, when Otto Kirchheimer (1966) drew attention to the rise of the new catch-all people's party, a more competitive model that tried to undo the old emphasis on strong representational links, seeking to exchange 'effectiveness in depth for a wider audience and more immediate electoral success.' These new-style postwar parties were to adopt a more aggressive approach to elections, attempting to win often short-term and contingent support far beyond the limits of their once pre-defined constituencies. They were also to become primarily office-seeking parties, with the desire to occupy government winning priority over any sense of representational integrity. Office mattered, as did electoral success, and the elaboration of party programmes, policies and strategies was increasingly attuned to this overriding competitive goal.

The changes in the forms of party politics that followed from the emergence of the catch-all party and its later successors, as well as the transformation in the patterns of party competition with which these changes can now be associated, may be specified under two broad headings: the *political identity* of parties, which has already been discussed in the previous chapter, in the context of party government, and their *location*, which is the main concern of the present one, and by which I mean to mark a process of *re*-location. The last decades of the twentieth century witnessed a gradual but also inexorable withdrawal of the parties from the realm of civil society towards the realm of government and the state, and together, these two processes have led to a situation in which each party tends to become more distant from the voters that it purports to represent while at the same time tending to become more closely associated with the alternative protagonists against which it purports to compete. Party–voter distances have become more stretched, while party–party differences have shrunk, with both processes combining to reinforcing a growing popular indifference to parties and, potentially, to the world of politics in general. This also becomes one of the sources of the growing popular distrust of parties and of political institutions more generally.

FROM CIVIL SOCIETY TO THE STATE: THE LOCATION OF PARTIES

Although there is some dispute among observers about how the recent transformation of parties may best be understood, and particularly the further develement from the catch-all party to the cartel party (Katz and Mair, 1995), there is consensus about the two broadly defined underlying processes at work here.[5] First, party organizations, however defined, are now less well rooted within the wider society; and second, they are

---

5. The cartel party is a type that is postulated to emerge in democratic polities that are characterized by the interpenetration of party and state and by a tendency towards inter-party collusion. With the development of the cartel party, the goals of politics become self-referential, professional and technocratic, and what substantive inter-party competition remains becomes focused on the efficient and effective management of the polity. Competition between cartel parties focuses less on differences in policy and more – in a manner consistent with Manin's (1997: 193–235) notion of "audience democracy" – on the provision of spectacle, image and theatre. Above all, with the emergence of cartel parties, the capacity for problem-solving in public life becomes decreasingly politicized and is less and less embodied in the competition of political parties.' Peter Mair, from a draft chapter for a book in progress with Richard S. Katz, *Democracy and the Cartelization of Political Parties*, for Oxford University Press (Katz and Mair, forthcoming). [*Ed.*]

also now more strongly oriented towards government and the state. Thus, if we conceive of parties as standing somewhere between society and the state – the most obvious approach to understanding their role and location within a democratic polity – then we can suggest that they have shifted along the continuum from one to the other, moving from a position in which they were primarily defined as social actors – as in the classic mass party model – to one where they might now be reasonably defined as state actors.

Evidence of the erosion of the parties' social roots is relatively easily adduced, and incorporates most of the trends already discussed. Electoral identification with political parties is now almost universally in decline, and the sense of attachment to party has been substantially eroded. Levels of party membership are now markedly lower than was the case even twenty years ago, and other evidence suggests that those members who remain within the parties tend to be less active and engaged. At the same time, the former privileges of membership have also tended to disappear, in that considerations of electoral success are now encouraging party leaders to look beyond their shrinking memberships to take their cues – and sometimes even their candidates – from the electorate at large. The voice of the ordinary voter is seen to be at least as relevant to the party organization as that of the active party member, and the views of focus groups often count more than those of conference delegates.

A tendency to dissipation and fragmentation also marks the broader organizational environment within which the classic mass parties used to nest. As workers' parties, or as religious parties, the mass organizations in Europe rarely stood on their own, but constituted just the core element within a wider and more complex organizational network of trade unions, churches and so on. Beyond the socialist and religious parties, additional networks of farming groups, business associations and even social clubs combined with political organizations to create a generalized pattern of social and political segmentation that helped to root the parties in the society and to stabilize and distinguish their electorates. Over at least the past thirty years, however, these broader networks have been breaking up. In part, this is because of a weakening of the sister organizations themselves, with churches, trade unions and other traditional forms of association losing both members and strength of engagement. With the increasingly individualization of society, traditional collective identities and organizational affiliations count for less, including those that once formed part of party-centred networks.

But this is not the whole story, for party networks have also weakened as the result of a sharpening division of labour, with the parties themselves often seeking to loosen their ties to associated groups, and to downgrade the privileged access formerly accorded to affiliated organizations.[6] In other words, the landscape has also been changed by the increasing tendency of parties to think of themselves as self-sufficient and specialized political organizations, ready to heed cues from any of the range of social actors, but preferring to remain unrestricted by close formalized links with them. Parties have therefore distanced themselves from civil society and its social institutions, and at the same time become ever more inextricably caught up in the world of government and the state. This process of party change has been fully analysed elsewhere (Katz and Mair, 1995, 2002, 2009), and need not be detailed again here. Suffice it to summarize a number of key developments that have marked most western democracies in the last decades of

---

6. A trend already noted *in nuce* by Otto Kirchheimer (1966) in his then highly prescient analysis of party development in the advanced democracies. For a more recent evaluation, see Poguntke (2005).

the twentieth century and since, and which look likely to be reinforced in future generations.

First of all, as is now widely recognized, parties in most democracies have moved from a position in which they were principally dependent for their organizational survival on the resources provided by members, donors and affiliated organizations, to one in which they now increasingly rely on public funds and state support, such that in most countries today, and in particular in almost all newly established democracies, the preferred source of party funding has become the public purse. This operates in a variety of ways.[7] One is indirect: the state may classify private contributions to parties as tax-deductible, so giving a major boost to a party's fund-raising activities; or may provide benefits in kind, such as free access to public broadcasting networks, or free mailings or poster sites. In most cases, however, and even in those few remaining systems where the principle of public funding is still viewed with some suspicion, state support takes the form of direct subventions for the work of parties in the parliamentary arena. These include funds for research and information-gathering, and for the salaries of researchers, assistants and secretaries who work for the parliamentary party as a whole or for individual representatives. Though often not regarded as constituting political funding as such, these particular state aids often provide significant help, either directly or in kind, for party organizations. And to the extent that more and more of a party's activities are centred within parliament, these funds play an ever more important role in specifying the party identity and defining its role within the wider political system.

---

7. For a recent overview of the patterns involved and the guidelines used, see Ingrid van Biezen, *Financing Political Parties and Election Campaigns – Guidelines*. Strasbourg: Council of Europe Publishing, 2003.

To an increasing extent, direct public funding is also provided for party central offices in order to help staff and maintain organizational work between elections. This sort of funding is sometimes couched in terms designed to depoliticize its intent, so that it may be provided ostensibly to promote membership affiliation among minority groups or younger voters, or for educational work that might facilitate citizen engagement, and so on in this vein. In practice, however, this has become a key means by which public resources are provided for partisan organizational and campaigning work outside parliament, and in this case also it has often become an essential source of income for the parties concerned.

State money is also sometimes made available specifically for election campaigning, and for party work at local or regional level. In this case, the justifications refer to the importance of parties in the democratic process, as well as to the need for voters to receive as much information as possible before polling day. Whatever the proffered rationale, however, the end result is that more and more parties in the democratic world have become increasingly dependent on state subventions for their organizational survival. Without this public support, it is likely that many parties would have difficulty performing their parliamentary roles, or even maintaining their extra-parliamentary presence. It is in this sense that parties have become dependent on the state, and appear as agents of the state.

Second, parties are now increasingly subject to new state laws and regulations, which sometimes even determine the way in which their internal organization may function. Many of these regulations and party laws were first introduced or were substantially extended in the wake of the introduction of public funding for parties, with the offer of state subventions inevitably accompanied by the demand for a more strictly codified system of party registration and control. Arrangements for party access to the public broadcasting media have also required a new system of regulation, which again acts to codify the status of parties and their range of activities. From having been largely 'private' and voluntary associations that had developed in the society and drew their legitimacy from that source, parties have therefore increasingly become subject to a regulatory framework whose effect is to accord them quasi-official status as part of the state. In other words, as the internal life and external activities of parties become regulated by public law, and as party rules become constitutional or administrative rules, the parties themselves become transformed into public service agencies, with a corresponding weakening of their own internal organizational autonomy (see Bartolini and Mair, 2001: 340).

The third and last aspect of this development is also perhaps the most obvious. Parties have also cemented their linkage to the state and to the public institutions by increasingly prioritizing their role as governing (rather than representative) agencies. In the terms adopted by the analysts of coalition formation, parties have become more office-seeking, with the winning of a place in government being now not only a standard expectation, but also an end in itself. Some forty years ago, a now-classic review of political developments in western democracies was organized around the theme of 'oppositions' (Dahl, 1966); nowadays, however, within the world of conventional party politics, there is less and less sense of enduring opposition, and more and more the idea of a temporary displacement from office. Opposition, when structurally constituted, now increasingly comes from outside conventional party politics, whether in the form of social movements, street politics, popular protests, boycotts and so on. Within politics, on the other hand, the parties are either governing or waiting to govern.

They are now all in office. And with this new status has come also a shift in their internal organizational structures, with the downgrading of the role of the 'party on the ground', and an evident enhancement of the role of the party in the institutions. In other words, within party organizations, there has been a shift in the party centre of gravity towards those elements and actors that serve the needs of the party in parliament and in government; as Maurizio Cotta (2000: 207) notes, 'those who control the government appear to be better able than in the past to also control from that position the whole party'. This shift might also be seen as a final manifestation of the classic Downsian or Schumpeterian notion of parties as 'competing teams of leaders', in which the party organization outside the institutions of the polity, and the party on the ground in all its various manifestations, gradually wither away. What we see is 'the ascendancy of the party in public office' (Katz and Mair, 2002). What remains is a governing class.

THE FUNCTIONS OF PARTIES

All of this has had major implications for the functions that parties perform, and are seen to perform, within the wider polity. As most students of party politics know, much of the literature in the field has laid particular stress on understanding the crucial functions that parties can be expected to perform in democracies.[8] Moreover, with some minor variation, there has been a remarkable degree of consensus about what precisely these functions are. Parties are seen to integrate and, if necessary, to mobilize the citizenry; to articulate and aggregate interests, and then to translate these into public policy;

---

8. Beginning with Almond (1960) and King (1969).

to recruit and promote political leaders, and to organize the parliament, the government and the key institutions of the state. That is, just as parties aimed to combine government for the people with government by the people, so too they combined key representative functions with key procedural functions – all within the same agency. Without parties, it was commonly argued, and without this combination of crucial functions, both the effectiveness and the legitimacy of conventional systems of representative government could be undermined.

In the main, however, the picture that has been presented in this approach to the understanding of political parties has also proved to be very static, being fixated on an image of the mass party as something both normatively and practically desirable. However, as parties have changed, and as the mass party model has passed away, the functions that parties can – or do – perform in contemporary politics have also been rebalanced. Indeed, as I will suggest here, the evidence points to the development from a time in which parties did manage to combine both representative and procedural functions to one in which they emphasize procedural functions alone. This development goes hand in hand with the concurrent relocation of parties from civil society to the state, and is therefore also part of the process by which parties and their leaders exit from the arena of popular democracy. Let us look at it more closely.

One of the first functions usually associated with political parties is that of helping to integrate and mobilize the citizenry in the polity within which the parties compete. This is, or was, one of their classic representative functions, particularly vital at a time when distinctions based on property ceased to be necessary qualifications for the right to vote, and the mass of citizens were first admitted to full rights of participation in the political world. In these circumstances, it became very important for parties not only 'to organize public opinion and to communicate demands to the centre of governmental power' but also to 'articulate to its followers the concept and meaning of the broader community'(Lapalombara and Weiner, 1966: 3). Party-led integration involved giving voice to previously excluded communities while also emphasizing their part in the larger whole. Today, however, such a role is more or less redundant, in that neither integration nor mobilization may any longer be deemed necessary, especially within the more advanced democracies. As Alessandro Pizzorno (1981) first suggested, this function has proved historically contingent. The bulk of the citizenry is already fully integrated, and has already acquired whatever political identity is deemed important. Indeed, the basis for contemporary integration and identity formation is in any case now more individualistic and particularistic, and hence less and less amenable to the traditional encapsulating strategies of political parties. Even to the extent that processes of mass integration or mobilization might still be seen as conducive to democratic consolidation – and this argument might be considered applicable to newly emerging democracies, or to the European Union polity – they are unlikely to be accomplished by either parties or their equivalents.[9] In sum, while parties may be important in other respects, this particular task no longer forms an essential – or even effective – part of their repertoire.

The second key representative function classically associated with parties is as articulator and aggregator of social and political interests present within the wider

---

9. This is also more or less what Philippe Schmitter (2001: 85) concludes after an assessment of the potential role of parties in consolidating third-wave democracies: 'Under contemporary conditions, there may be no way to get [the parties] right – if by "right" one means that they should be capable of ... playing a role comparable to that which they played in earlier processes of democratization.'

society. That is, parties give voice to citizens, and also create packages of policies in which various conflicts or incongruities in popular interests can be reconciled within coherent and competing partisan programmes. The aggregation of diverse but related interests into broad political programmes was always one of the key tasks of the traditional mass party, of course, but the articulation of interests was never their exclusive preserve, since this was also effected by non-party interests such as unions, churches, professional associations and the like. Nevertheless, at least during the heyday of the mass party, even those alternative associations and non-party movements that did serve to articulate interests usually operated under the aegis of party, or within the broader party-centred networks of representation. Indeed, this was the basis of traditional cleavage or 'pillarized' politics. In contemporary democracies, in contrast, the party and non-party channels of representation have become increasingly distinct from one another, leading to a new division of labour that has become one of the defining features in the patterns of representation in post-industrial democracy. This is especially true when the interests being articulated are more particularized and the channels of representation become more specialized and narrow-cast. In these circumstances, the parties have often aimed for self-sufficiency, and hence have relied less on their formalized links to non-party associations. At the same time, the various non-party associations have often found it preferable to compete for influence in the marketplace, and to play contending parties or political representatives off against one another. On both sides, therefore, the idea of a party-centred network has been proving less and less attractive or meaningful.[10]

---

10. The most comprehensive analysis of changing party-group linkages is to be found in Thomas Poguntke, *Parteienorganisatie im Wandel: Gesellschaftliche Verankerung und organisatorische Anpassung im*

But if the articulation of interests has often been pursued beyond party control, what of the more broadly based aggregation process? One possible reading of the changes that are occurring here is that while aggregation can still be considered important, in that at some political level conflicting demands still have to be reconciled, this can now be usually effected through the formulation of public policy and regulations rather than by means of a partisan programme as such. Rather than occurring within the electoral process, in which it is the parties in particular that would seek 'to organize the chaotic public will' (Neumann, 1956: 396), aggregation now occurs after elections, in the formulation of public policy and in government itself. Indeed, this was the key motif in much of the propaganda that built up around the 'Third Way' in the late 1990s, with government policies being designed to offer 'win-win' solutions rather than 'win-lose' alternatives (e.g., Giddens, 1998): when politics becomes non-partisan, this sense of representation, and hence aggregation, evaporates.[11] The contemporary equivalent of interest aggregation can also be achieved in yet another and even more depoliticized fashion through the delegation of decision-making to such non-majoritarian institutions as judges, regulatory agencies and the like.

In sum, party as such appears less and less necessary to processes of interest representation, aggregation or intermediation. The articulation of popular interests and demands now occurs more and more often outside the party world, with the preferred role of parties being that

europäischen Vergleich. Weisbaden: Westdeutscher Verlag, 2000. See also Poguntke (2005).

11. Note Tony Blair's remarks about 'what works' in an interview with Polly Toynbee and Michael White in the *Guardian* of 29 May 2001: 'I will always pursue political change in a way that tries to bring people together... We have become the practical party, pursuing perfectly idealistic objectives in a measured and non-dogmatic way.'

of the receiver of signals that emanate from the media or the wider society. These are certainly the terms of reference that were adopted in 2000 by the then Labour chancellor of the exchequer, Gordon Brown, when he rejected a trade-union proposal to restore the link between pensions and average earnings, a proposal that had just won the support of a large majority at the Labour party conference. 'I'm not going to give in to the proposal that came from the union leaders today', Brown declared. 'It is for the country to judge, it is not for a few composite motions [at party conference] to decide the policy of this government and this country. It is for the whole community, and I'm listening to the whole community.'[12] So conceived, the traditional representative role of the mass party eventually wastes away. Or perhaps it gets turned on its head, so that, as Rudy Andeweg suggests, 'the party ... becomes the government's representative in the society rather than the society's bridgehead in the state' – the party as spin doctor, as it were.[13]

But the work of social representation is not all that these parties did, or were expected to do. They also have a key procedural role, and here too there are two crucial functions involved. The first of these procedural functions involves the recruitment of political leaders and the staffing of public offices. If by this is implied that parties will always ensure the initial enrolment and socialization of potential political leaders, as well as their subsequent career path within the party network, then even this party function may have become hollowed out with time, in that parties in both old and new democracies seem increasingly willing to look beyond their immediate organizational confines when searching for suitable candidates and nominees. Indeed, with the

---

12. Quoted by Michael White, 'Angry Brown defies unions', *Guardian*, 28 September 2000.
13. See Andeweg (2000: 140).

decline in party membership levels, parties often have little choice but to look elsewhere, and, as the organizational strength and standing of parties diminishes, the candidates who are recruited are more often those who have achieved recognition in other fields. Parties in this sense have much less status or autonomy than before. Honoured in a minimalist way, however, in the sense that a party affiliation or party endorsement, however briefly or even opportunistically acquired, is seen as a necessary element in the election or nomination of candidates to public office, this function obviously continues to be crucial. Even Arnold Schwarzenegger felt the need for the Republican label in his successful campaign for the governorship of California.

Political patronage emerges as one of the key functions that parties still perform. Indeed, in certain political systems, where patronage appointments have grown in importance, or where, as a result of devolution in the United Kingdom, for example, the number of elected offices has increased, it might be argued that this particular function has become even more important. Parties have more positions at their disposal. However weakened party organization may have become, a party label remains a necessary acquisition on the pathway to political power, and within the institutional arenas of power themselves the actors are more and more likely to be professional – party – politicians, a strengthening trend not only for parliaments, but also for governments, with most European countries showing a steady decline from the 1950s through to the 1980s in the proportion of government ministers recruited through non-party channels (Krouwel, 1999: 210–15). Not only do parties still recruit, at this level, but they now seem to do so more extensively than ever.[14]

---

14. As Klaus von Beyme (1996: 153) notes, 'Elite recruitment [has become] by far the most important function in postmodern systems.'

The second procedural function that needs highlighting is that assigned to parties in the organization of parliament and government. This is potentially the most important function that they are required to perform, and yet, perhaps because of an American bias in the relevant literature, and because of the excessive attention paid to parties in presidential regimes, it is often overlooked. In systems of parliamentary government, the necessity for parties is self-evident. Governments in such systems need to be formed in the first place, often through coalition negotiations between potential competitors; responsibilities in government then need to be allocated across different departments or ministries; and, once formed, the maintenance of these governments in office requires the continuance of more or less disciplined support in parliament. None of these crucial tasks is feasible without the authority and organizing capacities of political parties.[15] Moreover, and even within presidential or semi-presidential systems, parties also facilitate the organization of legislative procedures, the functioning of legislative committees, and day-to-day agreements on the legislative agenda. There is little to suggest that the importance of this function has declined over time – and it is really only since the end of the 1980s that scholars in America have begun to emphasize its importance even on Capitol Hill (e.g., Cox and McCubbins, 2007).

The conclusion that can be drawn from this general overview of party functions is clear, and wholly consistent with the earlier assessment of the changing location of parties: the representative functions of parties are wasting away or being at least partly absorbed by other

---

15. For a comprehensive recent evaluation, see Bergman et al. (2003); see also Lieven DeWinter, 'Parties and government formation, portfolio allocation, and policy definition', in Luther and Müller-Rommel (2002), 171–206.

agencies, whereas their procedural functions have been maintained and sometimes become more relevant. In other words, the functions that parties do perform, are seen to perform, and are expected to perform, have changed from combining representative and governing roles to relying almost exclusively on a governing role. This is the final passing of the traditional mass party.

The key element within this transformation, whether seen in terms of the location of the parties within the polity, or in terms of the functions parties are expected to perform, is the ascendancy of the party in public office. Parties have reduced their presence in the wider society and become part of the state. They have become agencies that govern – in the widest sense of the term – rather than represent. They bring order rather than give voice. It is in this sense that we can also speak of the disengagement or withdrawal of the elites. For despite the rhetoric, it seems that they too are heading for the exits, although with this obvious difference: while the exiting citizens are often headed towards a more privatized or individualized world, the exiting political elites are retreating into an official world – a world of public offices.

The safe havens that are being sought in the wake of the passing of the mass party may be different; the withdrawal is mutual, however, and this is the conclusion that needs to be most clearly underlined. It is not that the citizens are disengaging and leaving hapless politicians behind, or that politicians are retreating and leaving voiceless citizens in the lurch. Both sides are withdrawing, and hence rather than thinking in terms of a linear sequence in which one of the movements leads to the other, and hence in which only one side is assumed to be responsible for the ensuing gap – the crude populist interpretation – it makes much more sense to think of a process of mutual reinforcement. The elites are inclined to withdraw to the institutions as a defence against the uncertainties of the electoral market. Just as state subventions to political parties have compensated for the inability of parties to raise sufficient resources from their own members and supporters, so the security of an institutional or procedural role can compensate elites for their vulnerability in dealing with an increasingly disengaged and random electorate. At the same time, citizens withdraw from parties and a conventional politics that no longer seem to be part of their own world: traditional politics is seen less and less as something that belongs to the citizens or to the society, more and more as something done by politicians. There is a world of the citizens – or a host of particular worlds of the citizens – and a world of the politicians and parties, and the interaction between them steadily diminishes. Citizens change from participants into spectators, while the elites win more and more space in which to pursue their own particular interests. The result is the beginning of a new form of democracy, one in which the citizens stay at home while the parties get on with governing.

4

POPULAR DEMOCRACY AND THE EUROPEAN UNION POLITY

The widespread drift towards forms of decision-making that eschew electoral accountability and popular democratic control, in Europe and elsewhere, furnishes us with a context in which the European Union's 'democratic deficit' may best be understood. Despite its evident idiosyncrasies, the EU should not be seen as particularly exceptional or sui generis, but rather as a political system that has been constructed by national political leaders as a protected sphere in which policy-making can evade the constraints imposed by representative democracy. The scale of the European construct may be unique and without precedent, but the rationale that underlies it conforms closely to current thinking about the role of non-majoritarian institutions, on the one hand, and about the putative drawbacks of popular democracy, on the other. To study the EU in isolation is to miss this wider, and increasingly relevant picture. The fact that conventional forms of democracy and representative government are difficult to apply at the level of the EU is not so much exceptional as symptomatic, and if the

Union could be democratized along such lines, then it probably would not be needed in the first place.

BEING SAFE FOR, OR SAFE FROM, DEMOCRACY

It is probably fair to say that the world is now more favourably disposed towards democracy than at any point in our history. By the year 2000, some 63 per cent of the independent regimes in the world, home to some 58 per cent of the world population, could be classified as democratic. Half a century earlier, despite the temporary optimism of postwar reconstruction, just 28 per cent of independent regimes, accounting for 31 per cent of the world population, had been classifiable as democratic. Further back again, in 1900, there were no fully fledged democratic regimes at all, with countries such as the United Kingdom and the United States combining widespread democratic practices in the exercise of public office with severe restrictions on the scope of the franchise. In fits and starts, or in what some have seen as more or less sustained waves (Huntington, 1991; Doorenspleet, 2000), democracy in the past one hundred years has therefore taken root and blossomed, and now flourishes widely. Small wonder, then, that the 1900s have been hailed as the 'Democratic Century'.[1] As Axel Hadenius (1997: 2) put it in his introduction to an end-of-century Nobel symposium, 'the principles of democratic government ... have been triumphing.' More important perhaps, by the end of the century these principles seemed neither subject to challenge nor capable of being challenged. 'After the fall of the Berlin wall,' noted

---

1. The term, and the figures, come from the Freedom House report 'Democracy's Century: A Survey of Global Political Change in the 20th Century', published on 7 December 1999. The full report can be found at http:/www.freedomhouse.org/reports/century.html.

Juan Linz (1997: 404) in the same symposium, 'no anti-democratic ideology appeals to politicians, intellectuals, religious leaders ... as an alternative to political democracy.' Or, as Linz and Stepan (1996: 5) noted, democracy was now 'the only game in town'.

But what sort of democracy was this? As recently as the 1980s, this might have seemed a bizarre question. Up to that point, and certainly during the peak years of the Cold War, the political world had been divided into three more or less simply defined categories: the first world, which was capitalist and also mainly, but not exclusively, democratic; the second world, which was that of the Soviet Union and China, and the rest of the Communist bloc; and the third world, which was courted and contested by both first and second worlds, and which was neither especially democratic nor powerful. Within this tripartite division, democracy was more or less just democracy, and while it was important for scholars and policy-makers to distinguish between democratic and non-democratic forms of government, and, especially in Cold War terms, to distinguish between different types of non-democracy, the democratic world itself usually remained undifferentiated. This view eventually began to change in the 1980s, at least in scholarly discourse, with the shift in perspective being facilitated partly by the so-called neo-institutional turn in political science. If the state was to be brought back in as an independent variable, and if institutions were to be used to explain individual behaviour and choice (e.g., Shepsle, 1995), then it was obviously going to be necessary to highlight differences between institutions and between various forms of democracy as well: otherwise there would never be enough variation to weigh in the explanations. The shift in perspective was also helped by the influential work of Arend Lijphart, who had initially sought to identify a distinct democratic regime type, consociational democracy, and who later, in a widely cited book, specified the various institutional differences that could be associated with the contrasting majoritarian and consensus models of democracy (Lijphart, 1984).

It was only after 1989, however, that the pronounced variation in types of democracy was brought to the fore. The former first world category, now ever more loosely defined, was soon filled to overflowing, and it became increasingly obvious that not all democracies were alike. Larry Diamond (1996) and Fareed Zakaria (1997), for example, soon drew attention to the contrast between the fully fledged liberal democracies that had long been established in the west and the more limited 'electoral' or 'illiberal' democracies that were then emerging in the former second and third worlds. Other scholars spoke of variations such as populist democracy or delegative democracy. Towards the end of the twentieth century, in what had by then become a hugely expanded field of study, the tally of discriminations had risen to more than 500.

In short, while the political field had become free for democracy and the democrats, as Linz had suggested, democracy itself was becoming less easy to define: the edges had suddenly become less sharp, the boundaries less clear. In particular, it seemed that it was no longer enough to define democracy according to its basic procedures, especially if the emphasis in those procedures lay with the electoral process and with notions of popular democracy. That had always been the key to the Schumpeterian notion – in which democracy was defined as a system that required 'free competition for a free vote', and embodied 'that institutional arrangement for arriving at political decisions in which individuals acquire the power to decide by means of a competitive struggle for the people's vote' (Schumpeter, 1947: 271, 269).

Now it seemed that something more than elections was required, or perhaps even something different. Echoing the traditional Madisonian or constitutional approach to democracy, various theorists and influential commentators began to downgrade the importance or centrality of the popular vote, and placed the stress instead on the need for institutional pluralism and for more reasoned or even expert decision-making. 'Elections are an important virtue of governance, but they are not the only virtue,' argued Fareed Zakaria (1997: 23), later adding that 'what we need in politics today is not more democracy but less' (2003: 248). Or, as Philip Pettit noted when clarifying what was entailed by his influential conception of modern republicanism, 'while democracy is certainly recognized as an important safeguard against governmental domination, it is never presented as the center-piece of the republican polity' (Pettit, 1998: 303). In other words, although elections and other modes of popular democracy remain important to the definitions of late-twentieth-century democracy, they are no longer privileged as guarantors of legitimacy. Indeed, if anything, it now seems that the structures of power and decision-making sometimes need to be protected from the people, and from excessive 'input'; that is, it seems necessary to create, in Everson's words, 'a sphere which is guarded ... from disruptive redistributive goals' and which 'serves the goal of democracy by safeguarding the democratically set goals of the polity from the predatory inclinations of a transitory political elite.'

THE EU POLITY

The European Union polity is probably pre-eminent among such spheres. To be sure, this is not a system that is wholly safeguarded from the inclinations – predatory

or other – of transient, or elected, political elites. But
by comparison with the conventional national political
systems of Europe, the scope it allows for organized,
electorally mandated input is notoriously meagre. This is
the case despite the fact that citizens seeking to exercise
control in and over the EU have access to two overlapping channels of political influence, with two sets of
delegates who may be mandated.

On the one hand, citizens seek to exert influence
through their national parliaments and governments,
and then, in a further step, through the Council of
Ministers and the European Council. Less frequently,
and less directly, they can also use this channel to
influence appointments to the European Commission
and other public offices at the EU level. On the other
hand, and with more immediate effect, but less weight,
citizens can seek representation through the European
Parliament, and here too, although again indirectly, they
can use this channel in order to exert a very limited influence on appointments to the European Commission. It
was through this channel, for example, that the parties
in the European Parliament forced the withdrawal of
Rocco Buttiglione from the proposed new Commission,
headed by José Manuel Barroso, in 2004. Although
constitutionally quite separate from one another,
these two channels nevertheless exhibit considerable
overlap, and this occurs in two important ways. First,
and increasingly, overlap occurs as a result of processes
of co-decision (or 'ordinary legislative procedure'),
whereby issues and/or appointments are decided on the
basis of input from both channels at the same time, from
both the European Parliament and the national governments. Second, overlap also occurs because, in the
main, it is usually the same actors or delegates that take
on the role of intermediary in both channels. In other
words, the same political parties, subject to control by

the same political leadership and by the same organized membership, compete in both channels. To be sure, the candidates and parliamentary leaderships that these parties nominate for election will usually differ from one channel to the next, and the labels under which they compete may also sometimes differ, since the campaign for the EU parliamentary elections may be organized under the aegis of trans-national Europarties. Whatever the label, however, and whoever the candidates, the key actors in both channels remain the national parties, and even within the European Parliament, the key principal for whom the MEPs act as agent is the national party leadership (see Hix, 2002).

As well as two channels of representation, there are also two dimensions of possible conflict and competition, having to do with the establishment and functioning of the EU polity and along which citizens and their representatives may be aligned. The first of these may be defined as that of 'Europeanization',[2] a dimension that is bounded at one end by conflicts over the institutionalization of a distinctive European political system (see Cowles et al., 2000), and at the other end by conflicts over the penetration of European rules, directives and norms into the domestic sphere (see Featherstone and Radelli, 2003; Goetz and Hix, 2001). That is, at one end of this dimension there exists the potential for conflicts regarding the creation, consolidation and territorial reach of authoritative political institutions at the supranational European level, whereas at the other end the potential conflicts concern the extent to which local policies and practices become subject to standardizing European influences and constraints. Here also is located a more complex set of issues, encompassing not only conflicts over the very formal aspects of Europeanization,

---

2. See Mair (2004: 340–43), from which the following paragraphs are drawn.

including the *acquis communautaire*, but also disputes over the more or less binding side-agreements that are reached by some or all of the member states with one another, and even over the convergence and standardization of cultural practices and lifestyles. Each kind of conflict requires and is dependent upon the other. Were it not for the institutionalization of a European political system, there would be little to exert an 'external' impact on the domestic sphere; and in the absence of any penetration into the domestic sphere, the institutionalization of a supranational political system would be of little practical concern. It is in this sense that these two aspects of Europeanization – institutionalization and penetration – are part of a single dimension.

This single dimension of Europeanization offers a close parallel to the territorial dimension specified by Seymour Lipset and Stein Rokkan (1967: 6–26) in their now-classic analysis of the development of national cleavage structures. At one end of the territorial dimension can be found those conflicts that involve local opposition 'to encroachments of the aspiring or the dominant national elites and their bureaucracies' (1967: 10); the European case is local opposition to interference from Brussels. At the other end are located conflicts that concern 'the control, the organization, the goals, and the policy options of the system as a whole ... [often reflecting] differences in conceptions of nationhood, over domestic priorities and over external strategies', and these, when translated to the European level, would be equivalent to the current divisions about the desired shape, depth and territorial extension of the European integration process.[3] The original Lipset–Rokkan schema also specified a functional dimension that cut across the territorial. At one end of this dimension were grouped

---

3. For a wide-ranging application of Rokkan's framework to the process of European integration, see Bartolini (1999; 2006).

various interest-specific conflicts over the allocation of resources. These conflicts were seen as pragmatic in nature and as capable of being solved 'through rational bargaining and the establishment of universalistic rules of allocation'. At the other end were grouped the more ideological oppositions, in which the conflict was not about particular gains or losses but instead concerned 'conceptions of moral right and ... the interpretation of history and human destiny' (1967: 11). This dimension too can be translated on to the European level. It does not involve Europe or Europeanization as such, whether specified in terms of institutionalization or penetration, but rather takes Europe as a given and divides instead along strictly functional lines, be these interest-specific or ideological. Conflicts that occur along this dimension take no position on the question of the EU as a polity, but are more concerned with the allocation of resources within whatever version of Europe happens to exist at the time.

Thus, there are two dimensions of competition involved here, one concerning the shape and reach of the increasingly institutionalized EU political system, the other concerning policy areas in which there is already an established EU competence, but in which there are disagreements about approach and priorities. Two dimensions and, as outlined above, two channels of representation: one working through European elections and the European Parliament, an institution which has an increasingly important voice and authority in the policy-making process, and hence on the outputs of the EU, but only a limited say over the constitutional structures or even over the appointment of the political executive; the other working through national elections and national parliaments and governments, that is, within the arena that has exclusive authority over constitutional questions. In principle, it should be possible to match the dimensions and the channels to one another, and, at least at first sight, it seems also obvious how they fit together. As far as opposition on the Europeanization dimension is concerned, for example, and especially opposition to the institutionalization of Europe, the competences of the various institutions are such that one would expect this to be channelled through the national route. It is here, and only here, that the relevant authority lies. As far as opposition on the functional dimension is concerned, on the other hand, while this might also be channelled through the national route, since some of the relevant authority is also located here, the expectation would be that this should mainly be directed towards the European channel, and through the European Parliament, since it is along this dimension that the main competences seem to lie. To be effective, therefore, representation via the national channel is best invoked for opposition along the dimension of Europeanization, whereas representation via the European channel is best invoked for opposition along the functional dimension (see also Thomassen and Schmitt, 1999: 258–60).

However, the real-world patterns of contestation tell quite a different story (see Mair, 2000). That is, when we look at the debates and programmes in each of the channels, we tend to find opposition regarding the institutionalization of Europe being voiced within the European channel, where no relevant competence lies; whereas opposition along the functional dimension is usually expressed in the national channel, even though authority on this dimension is shared with the European channel. The result is simple. The choices in both channels become increasingly irrelevant to the outputs of the system, and the behaviour and preferences of citizens constitute virtually no formal constraint on, or mandate for, the relevant policy-makers. Decisions can be taken by political elites with more or less a free hand. What we see, therefore, is the absence of effective representation in the European Union political system, in that, as with the various versions of late-twentieth-century democracy noted above, the citizens lack ultimate control (see also Thaa, 2001). Despite the seeming availability of channels of access, the scope for meaningful input and hence for effective electoral accountability is exceptionally limited. It is in this sense that Europe appears to have been constructed as a protected sphere, safe from the demands of voters and their representatives.

POLITICIZATION AND DISPLACEMENT

How can we account for this evident evasion of conventional procedures for popular control? In the short run, the answer, at least in principle, is very simple, and especially so when viewed from a supply-side theory of political competition: the system is driven by the choices made by party and political leaders when they contest elections, and by the strategies they adopt – in both access channels. That is, and again with few exceptions, political leaders dealing with Europe choose to contest elections on issues in which those elections cannot prove decisive, and to exclude those issues on which the elections can prove decisive.[4] They prefer to talk about the institutionalization of Europe when competing in elections to the European parliament, where

---

4. Although this is generally true for the mainstream parties in particular, the most extreme example of such displacement comes from the fringe, where the Danish June Movement and People's Movement Against the EU choose to fight their anti-European battle in the electoral arena of the European Parliament rather than in that of the Folketing. The two parties win a lot of support – they achieved almost 25 per cent in the 1999 round of European Parliament elections – but they are also clearly choosing, deliberately, to fight in the wrong arena.

it is largely irrelevant, and they prefer not to raise such questions when competing in national elections, where it matters. By organizing political competition in this way, these political leaders free themselves from any possible restraints imposed by external and binding mandates.

The result is a remarkable under-politicization of the Europeanization dimension (see also van der Eijk and Franklin, 2004). There may well be a potential for conflict over Europe – over its reach, its form and its sheer size – but, at least as yet, the parties that contest elections, particularly at national level, have seemed to want to leave this in the shadows. The preference appears to have been that Europe not be contested – at least within the mainstream. Cees van der Eijk and Mark Franklin (2004: 47) liken this situation to 'the sleeping giant', arguing that the European issue is now 'ripe for politicization' and suggesting that 'it is only a matter of time before policy entrepreneurs ... seize the opportunity ... to differentiate themselves from other parties in EU terms'. Indeed, it may be that we are now seeing signs of precisely this shift, and that questions of Europeanization are now beginning to more heavily assert themselves more forcefully in the various national electoral arenas.

This has always been the case in the UK, of course, where displacement has never been particularly pronounced, and where the European divide has long been a mainstream partisan divide. In France too, the issue has often come quite strongly to the fore in national elections, both parliamentary and presidential (e.g., Knapp, 2004). However, it is now striking to note how this pattern has begun to spread – to both the Netherlands and Austria during their 2002 elections, for example. Part of the reason for this, as van der Eijk and Franklin have emphasized (2004), is simply the increased salience of the Europeanization dimension as such – Europe now counts for more, and the conflicts it stimulates were further exacerbated by the lead-up to the 2004 enlargement and in the discussions regarding possible Turkish membership. Part of the reason lies also in the rise of new populist parties on both the right (mainly) and left (occasionally), and in the resentment and even hostility towards the established political class that can now be seen in a large number of European polities. (Table 5, overleaf) In this case, Europe has become a key issue with which to launch a populist assault, in that hostility to European integration has become one of the best possible weapons in the political armoury of the anti-establishment forces. Unlike the other issues – such as immigration – that also feature in the attack, it is one that unites, or is at least shared by, the outsiders on both right and left. In this sense, it can and does play a crucial role. This is hardly surprising, especially given that the long march towards European integration has always been a project driven by Europe's political and administrative elites; that is, it has been an 'elite-led process which has been largely unexplained and certainly under-advocated to the average citizen' (Bellamy and Warleigh, 2001: 9). Moreover, and largely by agreement across the political mainstream, it has also been a project that has been pursued without becoming politicized and without seeking to generate any fanfare. Indeed, if anything, it was to be developed by sleight of hand.[5] In the spirit of the so-called Monnet method, the EU-building process was almost always kept clear of conventional

---

5. This seems also to be the reading of Pascal Lamy, EU trade commissioner: 'Cooperation on coal and steel was the first thing the founding fathers of the European project agreed upon. It was a trick they played: they wanted a political union and the easiest place to begin was a common market in these two basic products'; see Joe Klein, 'Who's in charge here?', *Guardian*, 26 June 2002.

Table 5 Vote share of populist parties in western Europe

(a) general elections 1980–2010

	80–84	85–89	90–94	95–99	2000–04	2005–10
Austria	5	9.7	19.6	**25.9**	10	21.7
Belgium	1.1	1.7	7.8	10.8	13.7	10.9
Denmark	0	0	0	7.4	12	13.6
Finland	*0*	*0*	*0*	*0.5*	*1.6*	***4***
France	0.4	9.7	12.7	**15.3**	12.2	4.3
Germany	0	0	2	3	0.6	0.6
Greece	0	0	0	0.2	1.4	4.8
Iceland	0	0	0	0	0	0
Ireland	*0.3*	*1*	*1.6*	*2.5*	*6.5*	***6.9***
Italy	0.6	1.3	8.7	11	4.3	7.9
Luxembourg	0	7.9	9	11.3	10	8.1
Netherlands	0.5	0.7	2.5	0.5	**11.4**	10.7
Norway	0	0	0	0	0	0
Portugal	0	0	0	0	0.1	0.2
Spain	0	0	0	0	0	0
Sweden	0	0	0.2	0.4	1.4	4.3
Switzerland	3.4	5.6	8.5	5.0	1.2	0.6
United Kingdom	*0.1*	*0*	*0.2*	*0.4*	*1.7*	*4*

Notes: Where more than one election occurred in a single five-year period, the results are averaged. Here and also in Table 5(b), figures in bold indicate the best electoral showing for the populists in each national series. The figures in italic indicate the countries for which non radical right-wing parties are included, i.e., the June List and People's Movement for Denmark ([b] only), True Finns for Finland, Sinn Féin for Ireland and the United Kingdom Independence Party for the UK.

Table 5 Continued

(b) European elections 1979–2009

	1979	1984	1989	1994	1999	2004	2009
Austria	–	–	–	27.5 (a)	23.4	6.3	17.3
Belgium	0	1.3	4.1	10.8	10.9	17.1	11.2
Denmark	21	20.8	18.9	25.5	29.2	21.1	24.8
Finland	–	–	–	0.7 (a)	0.8	0.5	9.8
France	1.3	11	11.7	10.5	5.7	9.8	6.3
Germany	0 (b)	0	8.7	3.9	1.7	1.9	1.3
Greece	0	0	0	0	1.2	4.1	7.1
Ireland	0	4.9	2.3	2.9	6.3	11.1	*11.2*
Italy	0	0	1.8	6.6	6.1	5.7	11
Luxembourg	0	0	0	6.9	9	8	7.4
Netherlands	0	2.6	0.8	1	0.5	0	17
Portugal	0	0	0	0	0	0	0.4
Spain	0	0	0	0	0	0	0
Sweden	–	–	–	0 (c)	0.3	1.1	3.3
United Kingdom	0	0	0	1.2	7.5	21.1	22.7

Notes:

(a) The election was held in 1996 after the country joined the EU in 1995.
(b) The election was held in 1981 after the country joined the EU in that year.
(c) The election was held in 1995 after the country joined the EU in the same year.

adversarial politics and public political debate. Hence the displacement discussed above. As an elite objective, however, or as *the* elite objective, effective progress towards European integration could only be achieved as long as the elites themselves were trusted. This was the essence of the permissive consensus. It was a consensus in the sense that there was agreement more or less across the mainstream, and it was permissive in the sense that popular trust in the elites ensured deference to their decisions.[6] But once that trust and deference began to fade, and once disengagement and disillusion began to set in, the elites became vulnerable. And as they became vulnerable, so too did their projects, and in particular that for Europe.

This is not to suggest that European integration has now become a major issue of political dispute, or even a major cleavage. That would be a great exaggeration. But precisely because of the importance of the permissive consensus in the past, and precisely because that consensus so self-evidently concerned an elite project, the European issue has become a hammer with which to beat the establishment. This occurs not just on the right. The hammer is available to anti-establishment forces on both left and right, and both sides are happy to wield it. This new pattern of competition portends an increasing politicization of the matter of Europeanization, and hence also a possible breakdown of the long-term permissive consensus.

---

6. Note the typically acerbic observation by the late Ken Tynan in his 1975 diary: '6 June: Roy Jenkins, interviewed on TV after the result [of the Common Market referendum] was announced, made an unguarded remark that summed up the tacit elitism of the pro-Marketeers. Asked to explain why the public had voted as it had … [he] smugly replied: "They took the advice of people they were used to following".' See Lahr (2001: 248).

EUROPEANIZATION AND DEPOLITICIZATION

Even though its direct effect may be relatively limited, Europe exerts a strong indirect influence on the parties and their modes of competition, and in this regard its importance should not be underestimated. To begin with, the development of a European level of decision-making has clearly played a major role in the hollowing out of policy competition between political parties at the national level. This has happened in two ways. First, and most obviously, one major effect of Europe is to limit the *policy space* that is available to the competing parties. This happens when policies are deliberately harmonized, and when we are confronted with more or less forced convergence within the Union. That is, it comes from adopting the *acquis* and from accepting, at least in certain key policy areas, the rule that one size fits all (e.g., Grabbe, 2003). National governments may still differ from one another in how they interpret and act upon these demands for convergence, of course, and in this sense there may remain a degree of variation from one system to the next. But even when such interpretations differ across countries, they rarely appear to differ – at least across the mainstream – within countries. Thus even when one of the member states does seek to opt out of, or evade a particular policy, this usually happens by agreement between government and opposition, and hence the policy space remains restricted and the issue in question rarely becomes politicized.

Second, Europe limits the capacities of national governments, and hence also the capacities of the parties in those governments, by reducing the range of *policy instruments* at their disposal, and hence by limiting their *repertoire*. This occurs through the delegation of decision-making from the national level to the European level – whether to the European Central

Bank, or to Europol or to any of the many new regulatory agencies that now proliferate at all levels within the European polity (Kelemen, 2002). These are the so-called non-majoritarian institutions, from which parties and politics are deliberately excluded. In this instance, policy is decided according to a variety of different expert or legal tests of merit, and in principle, at least, is not subject to partisanship. If we think of parties and their national governments as armies being sent into battle on behalf of their supporters, then the effect of such delegation to Europe – as well as to other non-majoritarian agencies at national level (e.g., Strom et al., 2003; Thatcher and Stone Sweet, 2003) – is to reduce the amount of weaponry at their disposal, leaving them less and less capable of carrying through their putative campaigns. In addition, Europe has the effect of disallowing what had once been standard policy practices on the grounds that they interfere with the free market. Particular goods can no longer be excluded from import or sale, particular qualifications can no longer be deemed inadequate, and particular domestic services can no longer be privileged. Moreover, as companies such as the budget airline Ryanair have found to their cost, governments are severely restricted in the extent to which they, or other public authorities, can offer subsidies or help to particular industries or companies, and they are also limited in the exercise of their traditionally very basic function of determining which persons may enter and/or seek work within their territory. In other words, practices that involve public bodies in selection, privileging, or discrimination become more and more restricted, and hence the stock of policies available to governments, and to the parties that control those governments, steadily dwindles.

Both sets of limits serve to substantially reduce the stakes of competition between political parties, and to dampen down the potential differences wrought by successive governments. To be sure, elections continue to determine the composition of government in most polities, and as more and more party systems tend towards a bipolar pattern of competition, and towards a contest between two teams of leaders, this aspect of the electoral process is likely to become even more important. But insofar as competing policies or programmes are concerned, the value of elections is steadily diminishing. Thanks to the European Union, although crucially not only for that reason, political competition has become increasingly depoliticized.

There are two other senses in which the deepening of European integration can be seen to promote depoliticization and disengagement. First, there is the simple socializing effect, in that the existence and weight of the European institutions, and of the Commission in particular, is clearly going to accustom citizens to a more general acceptance of being governed by bodies that are neither representative nor properly accountable. The corollary of this is obviously that less attention need then be given to those institutions that are, contrastingly, representative and/or accountable. In other words, if important decisions are made by so-called non-majoritarian institutions, and if these are accepted and acceptable, then questions must be raised about the centrality, relevance, and sheer necessity of those institutions that still do depend on the electoral process. In short: politics is devalued to the extent that key decisions are taken by non-political bodies (see also Flinders, 2004).

Second, because the European Parliament – the one European body that does depend on the electoral process – fails to generate much commitment and enthusiasm on the part of citizens, it may well be responsible for a negative spillover effect in national politics. This can happen on the one hand through contagion, whereby a disregard for the European Parliament as a legislative institution, and in particular a disregard for the MEPs who work in that institution, can feed into, or be encouraged to feed into, a disregard for national parliaments and national representatives. If one elected body is seen to be ineffective and self-serving, then why not others? On the other hand, it can happen through a learning process, in that by not voting in European elections, citizens may learn that it is also possible and non-problematic to abstain from taking part in national elections. If voting is seen as a duty, then neglect of that duty in one arena may encourage neglect in other arenas, including the national parliamentary arena; and if voting is a habit, then even one experience of abstention may be enough to break that habit entirely. In other words, by democratizing the European Parliament, the polity-builders in Europe may have inadvertently contributed to devaluing the electoral process as a whole.[7]

If we put all of these factors together, what we see is that the reduction in the stakes of political competition at the national level, along with the wider process of depoliticization to which Europe contributes, acts to downgrade the real and perceived importance of traditional democratic processes: if politics becomes less weighty, then so too does democracy – at least in the sense of popular participation and electoral accountability. The result is not only the familiar democratic deficit at the European level, but also a series of

7. As early as 1981, just two years after the introduction of direct elections to the European Parliament, R.K. Carty (1981: 241) expressed concern about this very possibility, noting that 'it would be a tragedy if the net result of electing the European Parliament were a less democratic Europe.' It seems that the more powers the European Parliament has accumulated over the years, the less interest and support it has generated. See also Pijpers (1999).

domestic democratic deficits within the member states themselves. Because democratic decision-making proves marginal to the working of the European polity at the supranational level, it also tends to lose its value in the working of the various component polities at the national level. It is in this sense that, through the EU, European citizens learn to live with an absence of effective participatory democracy. They also learn to live with a growing absence of politics. For while European integration serves to depoliticize much of the policy-making process at the domestic level – by reducing the policy range, instruments and repertoire available to national governments and to the parties who organize them – it fails to compensate for this reduction by any commensurate repoliticization at the European level. It is true that some corresponding repoliticization can be seen in the growing evidence of contestation over the matter of Europeanization, as well as in the re-animation, through Europe, of formerly dormant regional or territorial lines of conflict.[8] As yet, however, this occurs only on a very limited scale, too small to count. Political conflict in this sense is being voided in Europe, by Europe. The question is: Why should this be the case?

THE PUZZLE OF APOLITICAL EUROPE

In the enormous and still growing literature on the EU system, one recurring theme concerns the apparent exceptionalism of what has actually developed in postwar Europe. In its most succinct form, this is encapsulated in the notion that the European Union represents

---

8. The reopening of the traditional centre-periphery cleavage in Norway in the context of the first EEC referendum is an obvious case in point (Valen, 1976), with more recent examples being found in Catalonia as well as in northern Italy.

a so-called *n* of 1,[9] a case to be investigated on its own, being neither a national state nor a conventional supranational or international organization, and neither part of the national political systems of Europe nor a distinct political unit in its own right. Above all, it is seen to be exceptional in that it lacks a 'demos', and hence, by definition – or so it is asserted – is a system that cannot function democratically: Karlheinz Neunreither (2000: 148) puts it baldly: 'There is no chance of a possible EU democracy, because there is no European people, no demos. No demos, no democracy – quite simple.' With time, of course, with education and with socialization, such a European demos might eventually emerge, and then it would become possible to speak of constructing a real democracy within what is now the European Union. Until that time, however, we will have to make do with something other than popular democracy, for it seems that 'without a clear sense of a European demos it is difficult to adequately institutionalize government either by or for the European people' (Bellamy and Warleigh, 2001: 9). What we have in Europe, therefore, is some strange and ill-defined polity, which, by virtue of the lack of definition, appears to be exempt from the standard tests applied to other sets of governing institutions (see also Gustavsson, 1998). If it is a non-democracy, it is because, in the end, it is a non-polity. This is also the lesson that Jo Shaw (2000: 291) appears to draw in concluding that the EU is a 'polity-in-the-making', for in such a context, she suggests, 'democracy remains both a conceptual problem and a practical challenge, requiring multilevel and multi-actor solutions that are "beyond the state" and, perhaps, also beyond the conventions of western style representative liberal democracy'. In these

---

9. See, for example, the debate between James Caporaso et al., *ECSA Review* 10:3, 1997, available at http://www.eustudies.org/Nldebate.htm.

terms, it seems that even the notion of a democratic deficit may be misleading, since it presupposes the application of inappropriate standards.

But for all its currency, this argument remains somewhat puzzling. To begin with, the assertion that the absence of a single, culturally coherent and presumably self-conscious 'demos' precludes the implementation of democratic solutions appears to fly in the face of all the attempts, both successful and unsuccessful, to establish democracy in multi-cultural or even multi-national territories. Indeed, even to raise this question is to invite a return to the classic early postwar discussions in political science about whether a viable democracy was possible in a culturally segmented or plural society. In that early literature at least, whether based on empirical data or theoretical argument, the answer was clearly yes: it was possible, even if the institutions of the democracy in question did have to be constructed in such a way as to allow for minority vetoes, cross-community cooperation, and what would now be called subsidiarity. In other words, it would be possible if the democracy in question were to be consociational, consensual or even 'working' (see Almond, 1960; Lijphart, 1977). It is precisely in such terms that Belgium, for example, which clearly lacks a single Belgian demos, or Switzerland, which lacks a single Swiss demos, or even Northern Ireland, which lacks a single British, Irish or even Ulster demos, can work with more or less standard democratic procedures and with the institutions of a fully democratic polity.

Even this is not the key issue, for if we also look again at the classic discussions in political science, and at the work of Almond (1960) and Easton (1965) in particular, then it seems hardly plausible to set the EU aside as something exceptional and incomparable. That early literature shared much with the contemporary literature on Europe in that it also struggled to come to terms with 'polities' that were not conventional states – polities in the making, or polities that were somehow primitively organized, or whatever. That literature also made major headway in seeking to extend the conceptual scope of political science beyond the limits set by its then more or less exclusive application to the developed political world and to what were seen as conventionally structured state forms (see Mair, 1996: 312–19). It did this in two ways. First, it sought to develop a new conceptual language that went beyond those conventional terms, becoming sufficiently abstract to accommodate the primitive, developing or so-called exceptional polities. This was the language of 'the political system', a language that allowed scholars to analyse the unusual and often poorly crystallized institutions that characterized much of non-western politics (Almond, 1990: 192), and that was able 'to encompass pre-state/non-state societies, as well as roles and offices that might not be seen to be overtly connected with the state' (Finer, 1970: 5). Second, it sought to relate this new conceptual language to more concrete and specific terms of reference in a fairly rigorous and systematic fashion, such that particular cases and institutions could be compared to one another at varying levels of abstraction. This was the approach that was outlined by Sartori (1970) in a now famous article, in which he distinguished between different levels of abstraction and specificity, and proposed a set of clear guidelines about how to move between these levels without at the same time stretching or abandoning the concepts involved. Adoption of this now-classic language and set of terms of reference has the advantage in this context of allowing us to treat the European Union as a political system, and, in this sense, as something that is comparable to other political systems.[10]

---

10. See also Hix (2004: 2–5) and Kassim (2003: 140–42).

That is, we can put to the European Union as a political system the questions that can be put to to any political system – and we can expect of the Union the standards of accountability and legitimacy that are expected of others. In this way, we can move beyond the limits imposed by assumptions of exceptionality. Whether the EU may be deemed a state is in this sense beside the point, since the purpose of using the concept of political system is precisely to avoid the confines of the concept of the state, and we do this by moving up the ladder of abstraction towards a definition that can more easily accommodate non-conventional political forms.

In other words, and following Almond (1960), the EU is a political system, in that, just like other political systems, it makes and implements binding decisions, and has the capacity to (a) extract resources; (b) regulate behaviour; (c) distribute benefits; (d) respond to demands; and (e) symbolize values and identities. Precisely how it does these things, or how it exercises these common capacities, may well be peculiar to itself, of course. But this is more or less true for any individual political system, and it is only through noting these differences that we can learn about and begin to understand the concrete cases that are to be found in real-world situations. Moreover, precisely because every individual system and actor is at bottom sui generis and unique, it is only possible to compare different cases by developing more abstract concepts with which to analyse and accommodate them. This is the essence of comparative inquiry: 'to substitute names of variables for the names of social systems' (Przeworski and Teune, 1970: 8). So, the fact that the precise form taken by the EU political system is sui generis, and that it may bear very little relation to the equally sui generis forms taken by the political systems of France, or Germany, or wherever, is not really important. It goes without saying that while

France, for example, is a political system, not every political system is France.[11] What matters in the case of the EU is that it is a political system, and that it can be analysed and compared as such.

So in what particular ways does this political system differ from others, particularly those in the European area? One way it differs is in its outputs, since in terms of Almond's list of the capacities of political systems, about the only output in which the EU has a pronounced role, as Majone (e.g., 2003) has often pointed out, is that of regulation. Indeed, for Majone, this is what makes it distinctive – distinctive as a state. The EU does not engage very extensively in the redistribution of resources, except perhaps via the structural funds; nor does it even do a great deal towards positive integration. But it is responsible for a substantial range of regulation, such that, following Majone, it might even be seen primarily as a regulatory 'state'. The EU also obviously differs when looked at in terms of its inputs, and this is clearly where the problems of representation and democracy arise. For, while in other political systems, and again particularly in Europe, inputs/demands are primarily voiced through elections and, within the electoral process, through parties, this is hardly the case in the EU political system as such. This is not to suggest that the system is unresponsive, however. On the contrary, it may even be said to be highly responsive – across its own institutions, to lobbyists, corporate interests, action groups, to individual citizens as well as other actors who gain voice through 'self-representation' in the courts and so on. The EU also sees itself as strong promoter of participatory governance, and clearly favours extending the involvement of

---

11. This paraphrases the observation by Sartre (1963: 56) in a more extended discussion of method: 'Valery is a petit bourgeois intellectual... But not every petit bourgeois intellectual is Valery.' See also Przeworski and Teune (1970: 17–23).

elements within civil society – organized groups, social movements, professional associations, stakeholders – in its decision-making procedures. Indeed, Beyers and Kerremans (2004) have recently shown that important channels of access are available even if they are used primarily by advocacy coalitions and lobby groups. But what is most striking about the EU when compared to other political systems in the post-industrial world is that it is not responsive in the terms of elections, parties and the conventional procedures of popular democracy. This is the core of the puzzle we are dealing with here, and it cannot simply be evaded by reminders of the uniqueness of the Union as such. What we have here is a political system that cannot adequately be reached or accessed by means of elections and parties, that is, by means of traditional representative organs and channels; a system that is open to all sorts of actors and organizations but more or less impermeable as far as voters are concerned; that cannot seem to work within the familiar conventions and modalities of representative government.[12]

THE EU AS A CONSTRUCT

In this lies the real puzzle concerning apolitical Europe: the point is not how to come to terms with something that is exceptional and sui generis – the issue of Europe as an n of 1 – but rather how to understand why the EU has been made that way. Instead of thinking about the forms of legitimacy that might succeed in a system that eschews popular democracy, it is more relevant to ask why popular democracy was eschewed in the first place.

---

12. On this particular issue, see also the conclusions to a wider study drawn by Thomassen and Schmitt (1999: 255–67).

In this context, the most important single feature to be borne in mind is that the EU is a construct, a system designed and built by constitutional architects. To be sure, like all other political systems, and like all other institutions, it has developed its own momentum. In this sense, while the EU may have been originally constructed in a particular way and for the furtherance of particular national or sectoral goals (Moravcsik, 1998), it has always had the capacity to go beyond this initial stage, and, as various neo-institutionalists and neo-functionalists remind us, it has long been a textbook example of how institutions can rapidly outgrow their original intent (see Sandholz and Stone Sweet, 1998). In this respect, it may even be said to have passed beyond control. But even to accept this is not to deny that in terms of its core parameters and institutional make-up, including all the modifications and extensions that have been built in the period from the founding Treaty of Rome to the present, we are dealing with a system that was established and approved by politicians who were both government leaders and party leaders. We may like to think of the EU as being somewhere 'out there'; but it is also sometimes salutary to recall that this is no deus ex machina, but something that is the result of hands-on moulding and shaping. The EU is the house that the party politicians built. The puzzle is that they built it without any substantial room for either politics or parties.

Why build a system of government that lacked conventional and familiar forms of democratic accountability? Even if we accept that this was not a problem in the early and very restrained stages of European polity-building, why extend the powers of an initially quite limited and bureaucratic organization without at the same time introducing some meaningful form of popular-democratic control? Given the recent growth

in the EU's remit, why continue to resist the adoption
of at least some elements of a democratically accountable presidential system, whereby the president of the
Commission would be subject to popular election, or at
least some elements of a classic European-style parliamentary system, whereby the right of nomination and
dismissal of the Commission, or even of its president,
would be in the hands of the European Parliament?
Given that a certain amount of power does now reside
in the EU system, why not allow its institutions to be
properly democratized?[13] There are at least three sorts
of answer to these questions, and we may look at them
one by one.

The first of these we have already considered in
noting the problems of the absent demos and the polity-in-the-making: the EC in the past, and the EU now,
are simply too exceptional to be suited to normal forms
of democracy. Indeed, why should we even consider
that democracy might prevail in these circumstances?
According to Erik Oddvar Eriksen and John Erik Fossum
(2002: 402), for example, 'the insistence on standards of
democratic governance is puzzling when considered in
the light of the widely held assertion that there is no
European demos, nor a genuine European-wide public
sphere.' In other words, while the practice of electoral
accountability and the logic of popular democracy are
all well and good when functioning at the level of the
nation-state, they are not really appropriate or applicable at the exceptional level of Europe. This is how the
theorist Albert Weale (1997: 668) puts it:

---

13. And why talk about the need to tackle the democratic deficit
while allowing it to worsen in practice?: 'On the record all core decision-makers are devoted to improving democratic legitimacy but institutional reforms are instead contributing to further diluting the link
between the citizens and the decision-makers in Europe' (Kohler-Koch,
2000: 513 [abstract]).

In many ways, the conception of democracy associated with the nation state, though tolerable in a way that it balanced competing values, was based upon a particular conception of democracy couched in terms of majoritarian popular will-formation through party competition. Since this version of democracy cannot be a model for an EU democracy (given that the conditions for its realization do not obtain), we need to reformulate the notion of democratic legitimacy itself in terms drawn from other strands of democratic theory.

Weale might as well have suggested, with greater bluntness, that if Europe doesn't fit the standard interpretation of democracy, then we should change the interpretation. Rather than adapting Europe to make it more democratic, we should adapt the notion of democracy to make it more European. That political leaders opt for a form of European governance that fails to match up to conventional democratic criteria is therefore a mark of their good sense: they know it cannot otherwise work or prove legitimate. The scale is wrong, the institutions are wrong, and the people – the demos – are wrong. Whichever way we look at it, the answer is the same: 'Democratic legitimacy within the EU cannot be obtained by modeling its institutions on those of the nation-state' (Bellamy and Warleigh, 2001: 10).

The second sort of answer sees the decision-making politicians as being motivated more by self-interest than by any sense of the common good. Thus, in one version of this answer, the reluctance to establish democratic institutions at the European level stems from an unwillingness on the part of national political leaders to encourage the emergence of any institutional competitors (e.g., Andeweg, 1995). It is acceptable to have second-order elections in Europe, it might be said, so long as there are still first-order elections at home. The opposite arrangement would obviously be much less congenial. At the same time, again for obvious self-interested reasons, although perhaps also occasionally for more altruistic motives, national political leaders will have been reluctant to contemplate democratic legitimacy migrating from their own domestic institutions to those of a new Europe. Indeed, it is this argument that sometimes drives British Eurosceptic rhetoric, and finds favour among senior politicians elsewhere in the EU. Nobody who has been in government wishes to be seen now as being in charge of a branch office. As I suggested earlier, however, such a strategy of resistance could prove self-defeating. Although Europe may not acquire much popular legitimacy if run in the Monnet way, its operations can still have the effect of reducing levels of legitimacy at the national level – not least by enhancing the various domestic democratic deficits. In this outcome – and if we can properly think of it in these terms – the sum total of democratic legitimacy is diminished and the position of national political leaders is weakened still further.

Self-interest looms even larger in another version of this answer, in which the attested tendency towards collusion among mainstream political parties, and the wider process by which party systems become increasingly cartelized, is markedly facilitated when policy commitments can be externalized to non-democratic decision-makers (see Blyth and Katz, 2005). Through Europe, as well as through recourse to other non-majoritarian institutions, politicians can gradually divest themselves of responsibility for potentially unpopular policy decisions and so cushion themselves against possible voter discontent. At the same time, they will take every opportunity to claim credit for policies that do win popular favour, even where these originate within the European institutions. However, this self-preservation strategy can work only when the institutions that

take over this role from the cautious politicians are
themselves not subject to popular control. Hence the non-
democratic shape of Europe today. That said, however,
there are other risks that arise in these circumstances,
which may not have been foreseen by the politicians.
To the extent that policy is externalized, for example,
politicians will be seen by their publics to be carrying
less and less responsibility, and hence will risk the onset
of what might be called the Tocqueville syndrome: that
is, an increasing inability to justify their privileges in
a context in which they fulfil fewer and fewer important functions.[14] In other words, if politicians choose to
divest themselves of responsibility by pretending that
they are only running the branch office, and if they go
on to feign helplessness in the face of the Brussels head
office, their status in the eyes of their voters will almost
certainly diminish. In this sense, cartelization may not be
a sure guarantee of success in the longer term.

The third sort of answer is perhaps the most serious,
however, and is also probably the most plausible: the
EU continues to be developed without traditional forms
of democratic legitimacy because these traditional forms
of democratic legitimacy no longer work. It is not so
much that popular democracy needs to be established
in the EU, but rather that the EU – along with various
less significant non-majoritarian institutions – is actually a solution to the growing incapacity of popular

---

14. 'When the nobles had real power as well as privileges, when
they governed and administered, their rights could be at once greater
and less open to attack... True, the nobles enjoyed invidious privileges
and rights that weighed heavily on the commoner, but in return for this
they kept order, administered justice, saw to the execution of laws, came
to the rescue of the oppressed, and watched over the interests of all. The
more these functions passed out of the hands of the nobility, the more
uncalled-for did their privileges appear – until at last their mere existence seemed a meaningless anachronism.' See Tocqueville (1966: 60).
For an earlier observation on this syndrome, see Mair (1995).

democracy. In short, the EU is not conventionally democratic, and can never be conventionally democratic, for the simple reason that it has been constructed to provide an alternative to conventional democracy. To repeat: if the EU were susceptible to conventional democratization, it probably would not be needed in the first place, In some ways this is quite a radical interpretation, but in other respects it is quite familiar. From the perspective of policy-making, for example, we know that the EU exists in order to make and implement decisions that cannot be taken or made sufficiently effective at national level – indeed, this is part of its appeal to many purposeful politicians (e.g., Lafontaine, 2000: 199). It offers both the economies and advantages of scale, and is seen as providing a more effective arena than the nation-state, as well as offering a basis for the 'rescue' of the nation-state (Milward, 1992). The Union exists to do things that no longer can be done – that no longer work – at the national level.

But there is obviously more to it than this. Were the EU to be simply a higher-level or larger-scale version of the nation-state, developing its own specific capacities within the context of a clear national – supranational division of labour, then it is likely that the pressure to democratize would become quite acute. If decision-making authority is being passed up the hierarchy, then so too should the conventional modes of accountability. Moreover, democratization in this context would be seen to entail quite normal procedures – that is, democratizing the EU would involve a core role for popular democracy, and would build on the model of familiar parliamentary or presidential institutions. Legitimacy in the EU, in short, would be derived in much the same way as it has been traditionally derived at the level of the European nation-state – through elections, procedures of accountability and, in all likelihood, through party democracy. This is clearly not what is envisioned, however. Indeed, in almost all contemporary discussions of the EU, as we have seen, it is assumed that 'normal' democracy can never be applied at this level, and that the means of deriving legitimacy cannot be modelled on the familiar practice at the level of national political systems (see also Thaa, 2001). Nor is this justified solely by reference to the still-uncertain boundaries of the EU: although the argument about the polity-in-the-making is a strong one (e.g., Bartolini, 1999; 2006), the rejection of conventional forms of democratic legitimacy goes much further than this. If anything, the eschewal of popular democracy and conventional forms of legitimation is the preferred option, and the EU wins favour as a polity precisely because it can sidestep these principles. It is not by chance that Europe was constructed as an alternative to conventional democracy.

For this reason also, however, the EU should not be seen as 'a special case' or as an exception. It can be better conceived as an outcome, or as the consequence of a longer developmental trajectory, in which democracy grows and mutates, and in which the mechanisms that allow democracy to function change and adapt. If conventional forms of democracy cannot be applied at the level of the EU, then, as I began by saying, this is not so much exceptional as symptomatic. On the one hand, it is symptomatic of the growing sense that the mechanics of popular democracy are increasingly incompatible with the needs of policy-makers; on the other hand, it is symptomatic of a post–Cold War world in which precisely because democracy is the only game in town, democracy itself – in the form of elections and electoral accountability – no longer needs to be defended, let alone promoted. For Fareed Zakaria (1997), the problem with elections is that they impose too strong a constraint on the capacity of governments to make decisions for the common good. Moreover, the electoral process can be seen to encourage policy responses that are more suited to the needs of those in power than to those of the society writ large. This problem can be avoided at the European level, however, since the EU is 'the place where the economic reforms that most of the individual members want, but can't do politically, are implemented'.[15] In other words, by this means it is possible to find policy solutions that are perhaps deemed necessary by governments or administrators, but that might prove unacceptable to many of the citizens of the member states and might be rejected by many voters. Besides, the EU and its related organs also offer expertise – something that, again, most politicians lack: 'Specialized agencies, staffed with neutral experts, can carry out policies with a level of efficiency and effectiveness that politicians cannot' (Majone, 1996: 4).

These and similar arguments tap into what is now seen as an ever-sharpening dilemma in contemporary political systems: the trade-off between efficiency and popularity (Dahl, 1994). What governments appear to need by way of policies is not necessarily what voters will accept – particularly in the short term; and what makes for a successful strategy in the electoral arena may not offer the best set of options for government policy. In the past (see, for example, Schumpeter, 1947: 288; Brittan, 1975: 136), this familiar problem was manageable thanks to the deference shown to governmental authority and the trust that was placed in political leaders. Voters may not have liked some of the solutions handed down, but they were more willing to accept them. Today, however, with a much more fragmented civil society, with more individualized and particularized preferences, and, above

---

15. Christopher Bertram, director of the Stiftung Wissenschaft und Politik, as cited in Joe Klein, 'Who's in charge here?', *Guardian*, 26 June 2002.

all, with government under the control of parties and political leaders that no longer seem able to serve as effective representatives and sometimes inspire little trust, other decision-making solutions need to be found. As Fritz Scharpf (1999, 188) has argued, 'even in constitutional democracies at the national level, input-oriented arguments could never carry the full burden of legitimizing the exercise of governing power.' Hence the raft of new non-majoritarian institutions, and hence also the growing powers and competences of those institutions that can operate beyond the democratic state – and the European Union in particular.

It is self-evident that European integration has been a problem-solving exercise. The full story is not only about economies of scale, however, for Europe is also problem-solving in the sense that it allows decision-making to evade the control and constraint of popular democracy and accountability. The key supranational institutions in Europe are non-majoritarian by definition, and although the Council of Ministers is at least potentially vulnerable to national democratic sanctions, it also proves evasive in opting to work mainly behind closed doors and in a non-transparent and effectively non-accountable fashion. The same holds true for the extensive system of committees – the so-called comitology – that bridges the Council and the Commission. As Deirdre Curtin (2004: 4) has recently put it, 'what has been qualified as executive [in EU terms] is on the whole depoliticized in the sense that it occurs outside of any public space of communication, deliberation and debate.' And the reason for doing this is that it is believed to get the job done.[16] 'Why is it that European policies which stagnate in the main political arena materialize in other shapes and forms elsewhere [in the

---

16. For a wide-ranging review of these issues, which is also more sceptical about the real capacity for depoliticization, see Flinders (2004).

EU system]?' asks Adrienne Héritier (2001: 57) in her revealing assessment of overt and covert policy-making. In this context the answer is very clear: it is because the room that allows those other shapes and forms to materialize was deliberately created when the EU system was developed, and this, in turn, was because of the a priori assumption that policies were likely to stagnate in the political arena. Politics and efficiency do not necessarily go hand in hand in this complex world, and, as Eriksen and Fossum (2002: 410) put it, 'extended participation and more publicity ... do not help much in reaching correct decisions in cognitively demanding cases.' But while this process may be built in to the EU architecture, it is nevertheless important to underline that it does not amount to a sort of constitutional equivalent of the policy-based 'rescue' of the nation-state. Particular policies may be rescued by transfer to a supranational or intergovernmental level, but democratic procedures are not redeemed in any comparable sense. In fact, by shifting decision-making one level higher, the architects of the European construction have been able to leave democratic procedures behind.

The EU is a solution to the policy problems and issues of credibility that have been confronted by decision-makers and their clients, offering a means of institutionalizing a regulatory system that would not always prove viable were it dependent upon the vagaries of electoral politics. On the other hand, it is a solution to the political problems posed by the failings of traditional modes of representation and party democracy at the national level. While lobby, NGO and interest group access can offer specialized and particularized alternatives to conventional party modes of representation, these often lack the general legitimacy they would need to take the place of partisan and electoral channels in the domestic realm – almost regardless of the standing of the latter. At the European level, by contrast, where the relevant partisan and electoral channels are notoriously weak, such particularized alternatives can thrive, so much so that, as Beyers and Kerremans (2004) suggest, it is often through such alternatives that European issues become politicized.

One consequence of the downgrading of normal democratic processes has been that within the European Union system itself, as well as in interested scholarly circles, there have been great efforts to redefine legitimacy so that it can accommodate the EU as a form of polity that is not conventionally democratic.[17] Fritz Scharpf's (1999) much-cited distinction between output-oriented legitimacy and input-oriented legitimacy can be read as one such effort. Another familiar and confidently theorized effort can be seen in Majone's insistence that the EU is simply a regulatory 'state' and, as such, does not require popular democracy: 'Redistributive policies can only be legitimated by the will of the majority, while efficient policies are basically legitimated by the results they achieve' (1996: 11).[18] Nor are such views exceptional. For Jürgen Neyer (2000: 120), for example, who builds on Majone, the European political system can be seen as 'a non-majoritarian regulatory apparatus', and 'the fact that majoritarian [i.e., popular–democratic] procedures are of utmost importance when justifying democratic governance in the member states does not automatically mean that the EC must also be democratized by means of majoritarian procedures.' For Thomas Christiansen (1998: 105), any increase in the weight of popular democracy in the EU, whether effected through a strengthening of the European Parliament or through

---

17. On this more general point, see also Katz (2001).

18. For a similar argument see Moravcsik (2002), who suggests that since the EU is just another – albeit very powerful – non-majoritarian institution, it does not actually need to be democratized.

expanding the role of national parliaments, 'would enhance the EU's democratic legitimacy. But it would jeopardize, at the same time, the legitimacy which the system derives from producing effective policy outputs.' And so on. Indeed, the contemporary scholarly literature is awash with the various current meanings of democracy and the many different nuances of legitimacy, such that almost any system of rule can be found to be acceptable – even that by judges and their equivalents. 'Expert-based decision-making is not on its own illegitimate and antithetical to democracy', argue Eriksen and Fossum (2002: 410). 'It is conducive to democratic legitimacy under certain modern conditions.' It is not surprising, then, that another, more immediately evident consequence has been the spread of popular discontent and scepticism, and the opening of a space that lends itself readily to exploitation by populist parties of both the right and the left.[19]

EUROSCEPTICISM AND POLITY-SCEPTICISM

The European Union political system is hardly anti-democratic: it is open and accessible to interest representation, it invites participation and engagement

---

19. It might be argued that the immediate problem here is that the constitutional architects of the European construct have not gone far enough in their abandonment of democratic legitimacy (see also Pijpers, 1999; Christiansen, 1998). By allowing a small opening for a fairly ineffective form of popular democracy at the European level – direct elections to the European Parliament – they have reminded at least some citizens of the limited role popular democracy plays in this whole enterprise. Had no such channel been created, popular acceptance of the non-majoritarian character of the EU might have proved easier to manage. To offer a touch of democratic legitimacy is to remind citizens of its limits; to offer none at all might well have facilitated the emergence of alternative sources of legitimacy.

from lobby groups, advocacy coalitions, and the rest, and its parliament is effectively – if not always intentionally – quite representative (Thomassen and Schmitt, 1999). But even if the system is not anti-democratic, it is nevertheless non-democratic, at least in the conventional postwar European sense of the term: there is a lack of democratic accountability, there is little scope for input-oriented legitimacy and decision-makers can only rarely be mandated by voters.[20] In particular, it is clear that the EU misses the third of the great milestones that Robert Dahl identified as marking the path to democratic institutions in the nation-states (1966: xiii). That is, we are afforded a right to participate at the European level, even if we may now choose to avail ourselves of that right less frequently; and we are afforded the right to be represented in Europe, even if it is sometimes difficult to work out when and how this representative link functions; but we are not afforded the right to organize opposition within the European polity. There is no government-opposition nexus at this level. We know that a failure to allow for opposition within the polity is likely to lead either (a) to the elimination of meaningful opposition, and to more or less total submission, or (b) to the mobilisation of an opposition of principle against the polity[21] – to anti-European opposition

20. [From this point onwards, the text follows the closing passage of Mair's 'Political opposition and the European Union', the *Government and Opposition*/Leonard Schapiro Lecture delivered at the Annual Conference of the Political Studies Association, Reading, April 2006 (Mair, 2007a). The original final paragraph and a half, making some twenty lines, of the 2005 version of 'Popular democracy and the European Union polity' has been excised, and the material now replacing it has been lightly modified for context. *Ed.*]

21. [Mair is invoking Robert A. Dahl's 'Reflections on opposition' (1965), which influentially distinguished three modes of opposition in western democracies: the 'classical' variety combining a challenge on grounds of policy with recognition of the government's right to govern; 'opposition of principle', which rejects not only the government and its

and to Euroscepticism. And indeed, this development is also reaching down into the domestic sphere, where the growing weight of the EU, and its indirect impact on national politics, also helps to foster domestic democratic deficits, and hence also limits the scope for classical opposition at the national level. Here too, then, we might expect to see either the elimination of opposition or the mobilization of a new – perhaps populist – opposition of principle.

Part of the problem here is that it is increasingly difficult to separate out what is European and what is national. In other words, as European integration proceeds, it becomes more and more difficult to conceive of the member states as being on one side of some putative divide, with a distinct supranational Union sitting on the other. Instead, we usually see both together and at the same time. Thus, for example, we have one approach in the literature on the EU which emphasizes how Europe 'hits home', while we have another and more recent approach that emphasizes how home – or the nation-states – 'hits Europe'.[22] In reality, each 'hits' and hence intermingles with the other;[23] the EU is also

policies but also the system of governance itself; and 'the elimination of opposition' in a situation where there is no meaningful difference between the rival candidates for political office – or in his own terms, 'government by cartel' (Mair, 2007a: 5). Ed.]

22. Tanja Börzel and Thomas Risse, 'When Europe hits home: Europeanization and domestic change', European Integration Online Papers 4:15 (2000); Jan Beyers and Jade Trondal, 'How nation-states "hit" Europe: ambiguity and representation in the European Union', West European Politics 27:5 (2004), 919–42. I also deal with this issue in Polity-Scepticism, Party Failings and the Challenge to European Democracy, Uhlenbeck Lecture 24, Wassenaar, Netherlands Institute for Advanced Study, 2006.

23. Thus, we might entertain what the great Irish writer Flann O'Brien might have called 'a molecular theory of Europe'. See O'Brien, The Third Policeman (London: McGibbon and Kee, 1967), where the molecular theory of bicycles is outlined in some detail. In brief, cyclists

the member states. But it in practice, it becomes difficult to separate out what is European and what is domestic; and if, in practice, the two become ever more closely bound up with one another, it then follows that dissatisfaction with Europe must also entail a more generalized 'polity-scepticism'. In other words, when we talk about Euroscepticism, and about opposition to Europe, we are also sometimes talking about scepticism and opposition towards our own national institutions and modes of governance. This is a scepticism about how we are governed, and it is, in my view, a scepticism that is at least partly fostered by the increasingly limited scope for opposition within the system – whether that system be European or national, or both at the same time.

This is also one of the reasons why our polities have now become such fertile breeding grounds for populism.[24] To a degree, this was foreseen by Robert Dahl

who ride their bikes often enough, especially on bumpy Irish roads, will transfer some of their molecules into the bike, while the bike will transfer some of its molecules into the cyclist. Eventually, the mix becomes so advanced that it becomes impossible to know which is the bike and which is the rider. On market days you might see old farmers who cycle a lot balancing themselves with one foot on the curb, or leaning with their shoulders against a gable wall, while late on cold evenings you might see their bikes edging closer to the fire.

24. [In a paper written shortly before his death, Mair (2011) drew attention to the systemic character of the populist oppositions and to a shared limiting tendency in their practice:

'... there are signs that the growing gap between responsiveness [to popular interests]and responsibility [to established norms of governance] and the declining capacity of parties to bridge or manage that gap is leading to the bifurcation of a number of party systems and to a new form of opposition (Katz and Mair, 2008). In these systems, governing capacity and vocation become the property of one more or less closely bounded groups of political parties. These are parties which are clearly within the mainstream, or "core" (Smith, 1989) of the party system, and it is these which may be able to offer voters a choice of government. Representation or expression, on the other hand, or the provision of voice to the people, when it doesn't move wholly outside the arena of electoral politics, becomes the property a half-century ago, when he talked about the decline of opposition and the 'surplus of consensus', and about the type of opposition that might develop in the western democracies of the future. Speculating about that future, he pointed towards the possible emergence of an opposition of principle, one that would be directed at the mode of governing itself. Not just the policies, and not only the personnel, but also the polity itself might be called into question:

> Among the possible sources of alienation in western democracies that may generate new forms of structural opposition is the new democratic Leviathan itself. By the democratic Leviathan I mean the kind of political system which is a product of long evolution and hard struggle, welfare-oriented, centralized, bureaucratic, tamed and controlled by competition among highly organized elites, and, in the perspective of the ordinary citizen, somewhat remote, distant and impersonal...
> The politics of this new democratic Leviathan are above all the politics of compromise, adjustment, negotiation, bargaining; a politics carried on among professional and quasi-professional leaders who constitute only a small part of the total citizen body; a politics that reflects a commitment to the virtues of pragmatism, moderation and incremental change; a politics that is un-ideological

---

of a second group of parties, and it is these parties that constitute the new opposition. These latter parties are often characterized by a strong populist rhetoric. They rarely govern, and also downplay office-seeking motives. On the rare occasions when they do govern, they sometimes have severe problems in squaring their original emphasis on representation and their original role as voice of the people with the constraints imposed by governing and by compromising with coalition partners. Moreover, though not the same as the anti-system parties identified by Sartori (1976: 138–40), they share with those parties a form of "semi-responsible" or "irresponsible" opposition as well as a "politics of outbidding". In other words, it is possible to speak of a growing divide in European party systems between parties which claim to represent, but don't deliver, and those which deliver, but are no longer seen to represent.' *Ed.*]

and even anti-ideological ... This new Leviathan [is seen
by many citizens] as too remote and bureaucratized, too
addicted to bargaining and compromise, [and] too much
an instrument of political elites and technicians. (Dahl,
1965: 21–22)

Political opposition gives voice. By losing opposition, we
lose voice, and by losing voice we lose control of our own
political systems. It is not at all clear how that control
might be regained, either in Europe or at home, or how
we might eventually restore meaning to that great mile-
stone on the road to building democratic institutions.

APPENDIX: A NOTE ON
ADDITIONAL TABLES

Tables 5 (a) and (b), in Chapter 4, are an editorial addition computing the vote share of a number of populist parties, for national general and European Parliament elections – from 1980 to 2010 for the former and from 1979 to 2009 for the latter. The parties featuring in the tables are mainly populist formations of the radical right, as defined by Cas Mudde (2007) in his seminal work on the subject, already cited in the draft text of *Ruling the Void*. They are accompanied by a number of instances that in one way or another deviate from the general pattern. The countries included are those of the European Union as it stood on the eve of the major enlargement of 2004, plus a number of long-established west European democracies outside the EU – a selection made to facilitate comparison with the tables in Chapter 1. Here, by country, are the parties included in the calculations.

- **Austria:** Freiheitliche Partei Österreichs (FPÖ) for the general elections of 1983, 1986, 1990, 1994, 1995,

1999, 2002, 2006 and 2008 and the European elections of 1996, 1999, 2004 and 2009; and Bündnis Zukunft Österreich (BZÖ) for the general elections of 2006 and 2008 and the European election of 2009.

- **Belgium**: Vlaams Blok (VB) for the general elections of 1981, 1985, 1987, 1991, 1995, 1999 and 2003 and the European elections of 1984, 1989, 1994, 1999 and 2004; Front National (FN) for the general elections of 1991, 1995, 1999 and 2003 and the European elections of 1994, 1999, 2004 and 2009; AGIR for the general election of 1991; and Vlaams Belang (VB) for the general elections of 2007 and 2010 and the European election of 2009.

- **Denmark**: the Dansk Folkeparti (DF) for the general elections of 1998, 2001, 2005 and 2007 and the European elections of 1999, 2004 and 2009; the Folkebevægelsen mod EU for the European elections of 1979, 1984, 1989, 1994, 1999, 2004 and 2009; and the JuniBevægelsen for the European elections of 1994, 1999, 2004 and 2009. The last two organizations are examples of cross-party populist and Eurosceptical movements.

- **Finland**: There are no significant populist radical right-wing parties as such competing at the national level in Finland. A populist and nationalist party sharing traits of both the left and the right has existed since 1995, with the True Finns backing both left-wing economic policies and a conservative stance on social issues. Their results are included for the general elections of 1999, 2003 and 2007 and for the European elections of 1996, 1999, 2004 and 2009.

- **France**: Front National (FN) for the general elections of 1981, 1986, 1988, 1993, 1997, 2002 and 2007 and the European elections of 1979, 1984, 1989, 1994, 1999, 2004 and 2009; and the Mouvement National Républicain (MNR) for the general election of 2002.

- **Germany:** Republikaner (REP) for the general elections of 1990, 1994, 1998, 2002, 2005, 2007 and 2009 and the European elections of 1989, 1994, 1999, 2004 and 2009; Deutsche Volksunion (DVU) for the general election of 1998 and the European election of 1989.

- **Greece:** Front Line (FL) for the general election of 2000; Party of Hellenism (KE) for the 1996 and 2000 general elections and the European election of 1999; Hellenic Front (EM) for the general election of 2000 and the European election of 1999; Laikos Orthodoxos Synagermos (LAOS) for the general elections of 2004, 2007 and 2009 and the European elections of 2004 and 2009.

- **Iceland:** there are no significant populist radical right-wing parties competing at the national level in Iceland.

- **Ireland:** there are no significant populist radical right-wing parties competing at the national level in Ireland. Sinn Féin, historically a nationalist party, may be seen as representing a kind of left-wing populism, especially in its Eurosceptical stance. Sinn Féin's results are included for the general elections of 1992, 1997, 2002 and 2007 and for the European elections of 1984, 1989, 1994, 1999, 2004 and 2009.

- **Italy:** Lega Lombarda (LL) for the general elections of 1983, 1987 and 1992 and the European election of 1989; Liga Veneta (LV) for the general elections of 1983 and 1987; Movimento Sociale – Fiamma Tricolore for the general elections of 1996, 2001, 2006 and 2008 and the European elections of 1999, 2004 and 2009; Lega Nord for the general elections of 1994, 1996, 2001, 2006 and 2008 and the European elections of 1994, 1999, 2004 and 2009.

- **Luxembourg:** Aktiounskomitee fir Demokratie a Rentegerechtegkeet (ADR) for the general elections of

1989, 1994, 1999, 2004 and 2009 and the European elections of 1994, 1999, 2004 and 2009.

- **Netherlands:** Nederlandse Volksunie (NVU) for the general election of 1981; Centrumpartij (CP) for the general elections of 1981, 1982 and 1986 and the European election of 1984; Centrumdemocraten for the general elections of 1986 and 1994 and the European elections of 1989, 1994 and 1999; Partij voor de Vrijheid (PVV) for the general elections of 2006 and 2010 and the European election of 2009; Lijst Pim Fortuyn (LPF) for the general election of 2002.
- **Norway:** there are no significant populist radical right-wing parties competing at the national level in Norway.
- **Portugal:** Partido Renovador Nacional (PRN) for the general elections of 2002, 2005 and 2009.
- **Spain:** there are no significant populist radical-right parties competing at the national level in Spain.
- **Sweden:** Sverigedemokraterna (SD) for the general elections of 1991, 1994, 1998, 2002, 2006 and 2010 and the European elections of 1999, 2004 and 2009.
- **Switzerland:** Nationale Aktion für Volk und Heimat (NA) for the general election of 1983; Freiheits-Partei der Schweiz/Parti Suisse de la liberté (FPS/PSL) for the general elections of 1987, 1991, 1995, 1999, 2003 and 2007; Schweizer Demokraten/Démocrates suisses (SD) for the general elections of 1987, 1991, 1995, 1999, 2003 and 2007.
- **United Kingdom:** National Front (NF) for the general elections of 1983 and 1992; British National Party (BNP) for the general elections of 1992, 1997, 2001, 2005 and 2010 and the European elections of 1999, 2004 and 2009; United Kingdom Independence Party (UKIP) for the general elections of 1997, 2001, 2005 and 2010 and the European elections of 1994, 1999,

2004 and 2009. (UKIP differs from a radical-right-wing organization such as the BNP in its concern for mainstream respectability but certainly displays many populist traits.)

SOURCES

NSD European Election Database:
http://www.nsd.uib.no/european_election_database/
IPU Parline Database on National Parliaments:
http://www.ipu.org/parline/parlinesearch.asp
Parlgov Database:
http://parlgov.org/stable/index.html
Psephos – Adam Carr's Election Archive:
http://psephos.adam-carr.net/
Adele archive of the Istituto Cattaneo:
http://www.cattaneo.org/index.asp?l1=archivi&l2=adele
Election data of the Spanish Interior Ministry:
http://www.infoelectoral.mir.es

BIBLIOGRAPHY

Almond, Gabriel A. 1960. Introduction: a functional approach to comparative politics. In *The Politics of Developing Areas*, edited by Gabriel A. Almond and James S. Coleman. Princeton: Princeton University Press.

Almond, Gabriel A. 1990. *A Discipline Divided*. London: Sage.

Andeweg, Rudy B. 1995. The reshaping of national party systems. *West European Politics* 18 (3): 58–78.

Andeweg, R.B. 1996. Elite-mass linkages in Europe: legitimacy crisis or party crisis? In *Elitism, Populism and European Politics*, edited by J. Hayward. Oxford: Clarendon Press, 143–63.

Andeweg, Rudy B. 2000. Political recruitment and party government. In *The Nature of Party Government: A Comparative European Perspective*, edited by Jean Blondel and Maurizio Cotta. Basingstoke: Palgrave, 38–55.

Anon. 1950. *Towards a More Responsible Two-Party System*. New York: Report of the APSA Committee on the Political Parties.

Bagehot, Walter. 1963. *The English Constitution*. London: Collins.

Bale, Tim. 2003. Cinderella and her ugly sisters: the mainstream and extreme right in Europe's bipolarising party systems. *West European Politics* 26 (3): 67–90.

Bartolini, Stefano, and Peter Mair. 1990. *Identity, Competition and Electoral Availability: The Stabilisation of European Electorates, 1885–1985.* Cambridge: Cambridge University Press.

Bartolini, Stefano. 1999. Political representation in loosely bounded territories: between Europe and the nation-state. Paper presented to the conference on Multi-level party systems: Europeanization and the reshaping of national political representation, December, European University Institute, Florence.

Bartolini, Stefano. 2000. *The Political Mobilization of the European Left, 1860–1980: The Class Cleavage.* Cambridge: Cambridge University Press.

Bartolini, Stefano, and Peter Mair. 2001. Challenges to contemporary political parties. In *Political Parties and Democracy*, edited by Larry Diamond and Richard Gunther. Baltimore: Johns Hopkins University, 327–45.

Bartolini, Stefano. 2006. *Re-Structuring Europe: Centre formation, System-Building and Political Structuring Between the Nation State and the European Union.* Oxford: Oxford University Press.

Beck, Ulrich. 1992. *Risk Society: Towards a New Modernity.* London: SAGE.

Bellamy, Richard, and Alex Warleigh. 2001. Introduction: the puzzle of EU citizenship. In *Citizenship and Governance in the European Union*, edited by Richard Bellamy and Alex Warleigh. London: Continuum, 1–12.

Bennett, W. Lance. 1998. The uncivic culture: communication, identity, and the rise of lifestyle politics. *PS: Political Science and Politics*, 31 (4): 740–61.

Berger, Suzanne. 1979. Politics and antipolitics in Western Europe in the seventies. *Daedalus* 108 (1): 27–50.

Bergman, Torbjörn, Wolfgang C. Müller, Kaare Strøm and Magnus Blomgren. 2003. Democratic delegation and accountability: cross-national patterns. In *Delegation and Accountability in Parliamentary Democracies*, edited by

Kaare Strom, Wolfgang C. Muller and Torbjørn Bergman. Oxford: Oxford University Press, 109–220.

Best, Robin E. 2011. The declining electoral relevance of traditional cleavage groups. *European Political Science Review* 3 (2): 279–300.

Beyers, Jan, and Bert Kerremans. 2004. Bureaucrats, politicians, and societal interests: How is European policy-making politicized? *Comparative Political Studies* 37 (10): 1119–51.

Beyers, Jan, and Jade Trondal. 2000. How nation-states 'hit' Europe: ambiguity and representation in the European Union. *West European Politics* 27 (5): 919–42.

Beyme, Klaus von. 1996. Party leadership and change in party systems: towards a postmodern party state? *Government and Opposition* 31 (2): 35–59.

Blinder, Alan S. 1997. Is government too political? *Foreign Affairs* (November/December): 115–26.

Blondel, Jean, and Maurizio Cotta. 2000. *The Nature of Party Government: A Comparative European Perspective.* Houndmills, Basingstoke: Palgrave Macmillan.

Blyth, Mark, and Richard S. Katz. 2005. From catch-all politics to cartelization: the political economy of the cartel party. *West European Politics* 28 (1): 33–60.

Boix, Carles. 1998. *Political Parties, Growth and Equality: Conservative and Social Democratic Economic Strategies in the World Economy.* Cambridge: Cambridge University Press.

Börzel, Tanja, and Thomas Risse. 2000. When Europe hits home: Europeanization and domestic change. *European Integration Online Papers.* 4 (15).

Brittan, Samuel. 1975. The economic contradictions of democracy. *British Journal of Political Science* 5 (2): 129–259.

Carty, R.K. 1981. Towards a European politics: the lessons of the European Parliament election in Ireland. *Journal of European Integration* 4 (2): 211–42.

Carty, R.K. 2002. Canada's nineteenth-century cadre parties at the millennium. In *Political Parties in Advanced Industrial Democracies*, edited by Paul Webb, David Farrell and Ian Holliday. Oxford: Oxford University Press, 345–79.

Castles, Francis Geoffrey. 1982. *The Impact of Parties: Politics and Policies in Democratic Capitalist States*. London: Sage Publications.

Caul, Miki, and Mark M. Gray. 2000. From platform declarations to policy outcomes: changing party profiles and partisan influence over policy. In *Parties Without Partisans: Political Change in Advanced Industrial Democracies*, edited by Russell J. Dalton and Martin P. Wattenberg. Oxford: Oxford University Press, 208–37.

Christiansen, Thomas. 1998. Legitimacy dilemmas of supranational governance: the European Commission between accountability and independence. In *Political Theory and the European Union: Legitimacy, Constitutional Choice and Citizenship*, edited by Albert Weale and Michael Nentwich. London: Routledge, 97–110.

Chua, Amy. 2003. *World on Fire: How Exporting Free Market Democracy Breeds Ethnic Hatred and Global Instability*. New York: Doubleday.

Collier, David, and Steven Levitsky. 1997. Democracy with adjectives: conceptual innovations in comparative research. *World Politics* 49 (3): 430–51.

Cotta, Maurizio. 2000. Conclusion: from the simple world of party government to a more complex view of party-government relationships. In *The Nature of Party Government: A Comparative European Perspective*, edited by Jean Blondel and Maurizio Cotta. Basingstoke: Palgrave, 196–222.

Cotta, Maurizio, and Heinrich Best. 2000. Between professionalization and democratization: a synoptic view on the making of the European representative. In *Parliamentary Representatives in Europe 1848–2000: Legislative Recruitment and Careers in Eleven European Countries*, edited by Heinrich Best and Maurizio Cotta. Oxford: Oxford University Press, 493–525.

Cowles, Maria Green, James Caporaso and Thomas Risse, eds. 2001. *Transforming Europe: Europeanization and Domestic Change*. Ithaca: Cornell University Press.

Cox, Gary W., and Mathew Daniel McCubbins. 2007. *Legislative Leviathan: Party Government in the House*. Cambridge: Cambridge University Press.

Curtin, Deirdre. 2004. The evolving legal and institutional practices of the Council of Ministers: public access to (digital) information and the public sphere. Unpublished manuscript.

Daalder, Hans. 1987. Countries in comparative European politics. *European Journal of Political Research* 15 (1): 3–21.

Dahl, Robert A. 1956. *A Preface to Democratic Theory*. Chicago: University of Chicago Press.

Dahl, Robert A. 1965. Reflections on opposition in western democracies. *Government and Opposition* 1 (1): 7–24.

Dahl, Robert A. 1966. *Political Oppositions in Western Democracies*, edited by Robert A. Dahl. New Haven: Yale University Press.

Dahl, Robert A. 1994. A democratic dilemma: system effectiveness versus citizen participation. *Political Science Quarterly* 109 (1): 23–34.

Dahl, Robert A. 1999. *The Past and Future of Democracy*. Occasional Paper Number 5, Centre for the Study of Political Change, University of Siena.

Dalton, Russell J., Scott C. Flanagan, Paul Allen Beck and James E. Alt. 1984. *Electoral Change in Advanced Industrial Democracies: Realignment or Dealignment?* Princeton: Princeton University Press.

Dalton, Russell J. 2000. The decline of party identification. In *Parties Without Partisans: Political Change in Advanced Industrial Democracies*, edited by Russell J. Dalton and Martin P. Wattenberg, Oxford: Oxford University Press, 19–36.

Dalton, Russell J., and Martin P. Wattenberg. 2000. *Parties Without Partisans: Political Change in Advanced Industrial Democracies*. Oxford: Oxford University Press.

Dalton, Russell J. 2004. *Democratic Challenges, Democratic Choices: The Erosion of Political Support in Advanced Industrial Democracies*. Oxford: Oxford University Press.

DeWinter, Lieven. 2002. Parties and government formation, portfolio allocation, and policy definition. In *Political Parties in the New Europe*, edited by Kurt Richard Luther and Ferdinand Müller-Rommel, Oxford: Oxford University Press, 171–206.

Diamond, Larry. 1996. Is the third wave over? *Journal of Democracy* 7 (3): 20–37.

Doorenspleet, Renske. 2000. Reassessing the three waves of democratization. *World Politics* 52 (3): 384–406.

Downs, William M. 2001. Pariahs in their midst: Belgian and Norwegian parties react to extremist threats. *West European Politics* 24 (3): 23–42.

Easton, David. 1965. *A Systems Analysis of Political Life*. New York: Wiley.

Eijk, Cees van der, and Mark Franklin. 2004. Potential for contestation on European matters at national elections in Europe. In *European Integration and Political Conflict*, edited by Gary Marks and Marco R. Steenbergen. Cambridge: Cambridge University Press, 32–50.

Eisenstadt, S.N. 1999. *Paradoxes of Democracy: Fragility, Continuity, and Change*. Washington, DC: Woodrow Wilson Center Press/Johns Hopkins University Press.

Elff, Martin. 2007. Social structure and electoral behavior in comparative perspective: the decline of social cleavages in Western Europe revisited. *Perspectives on Politics* 5 (2): 277–94.

Eriksen, Erik Oddvar, and John Erik Fossum. 2002. Democracy through strong publics in the European Union. *Journal of Common Market Studies* 40 (3): 401–24.

Everson, Michelle. 2000. Beyond the Bundesverfassungsgericht: on the necessary cunning of constitutional reasoning, in *The European Union and Its Order: The Legal Theory of European Integration*, edited by Zenon Bankowski and Andrew Scott. Oxford: Blackwell, 91–112.

Featherstone, Kevin, and Claudio M. Radaelli, eds. 2003. *The Politics of Europeanization*. Oxford: Oxford University Press.

Finer, S.E. 1970. Almond's concept of the political system. *Government and Opposition* 5 (1): 3–21.

Finer, S.E. 1975. *Adversary Politics and Electoral Reform*.

Flinders, Matthew. 2004. Distributed public governance in the European Union. *Journal of European Public Policy* 11 (3): 520–44.

Flinders, Matthew, and Jim Buller. 2004. Depoliticization, democracy, and arena-shifting. Unpublished paper.

Franklin, Mark N. 2002. The dynamics of electoral participation. In *Comparing Democracies 2: New Challenges in the Study of Elections and Voting*, edited by Lawrence LeDuc, Richard G. Niemi and Pippa Norris. London: SAGE, 148–67.

Franklin, Mark N. 2004. *Voter Turnout and the Dynamics of Electoral Competition in Established Democracies Since 1945*. Cambridge: Cambridge University Press.

Franklin, Mark N., Thomas T. Mackie and Henry Valen, eds. 1992. *Electoral Change: Responses to Evolving Social and Attitudinal Structures in Western Countries*. Cambridge: Cambridge University Press.

Garrett, Geoffrey. 1998. *Partisan Politics in the Global Economy*. Cambridge: Cambridge University Press.

Garrett, Geoffrey. 2000. Globalization and government spending around the world. Working Paper 2000/155. Madrid: Istituto Juan March.

Giddens, Anthony. 1998. *The Third Way: The Renewal of Social Democracy*. London: Polity Press.

Goetz, Klaus H., and Simon Hix, eds. 2001. *Europeanised Politics? European Integration and National Political Systems*. London: Cass.

Grabbe, Heather. 2003. Europeanization goes east: power and uncertainty in the EU accession process. In *The Politics of Europeanization*, edited by Kevin Featherstone and Claudio M. Radaelli. Oxford: Oxford University Press, 303–30.

Gustavsson, Sverker. 1998. Defending the democratic deficit, in *Political Theory and the European Union: Legitimacy, Constitutional Choice and Citizenship*, edited by Albert Weale and Michael Nentwich. London: Routledge, 65–80.

Hadenius, Axel. 1997. Victory and crisis: introduction. In *Democracy's Victory and Crisis: Nobel Symposium No. 93*, edited by Axel Hadenius. Cambridge: Cambridge University Press, 1–14.

Hardin, Russell. 2000. The public trust. In *Disaffected Democracies: What's Troubling the Trilateral Countries?*, edited by Susan J. Pharr and Robert D. Putnam. Cambridge: Cambridge University Press, 31–51.

Heinisch, Reinhard. 2003. Success in opposition – failure in government: explaining the performance of right-wing populist parties in public office. *West European Politics* 26 (3): 91–130.

Héritier, Adrienne. 2001. Overt and covert institutionalization in Europe. In *The Institutionalization of Europe*, edited by Alec Stone Sweet, Wayne Sandholtz and Neil Fligstein. Oxford: Oxford University Press, 56–70.

Hix, Simon. 2002. Parliamentary behavior with two principals: preferences, parties, and voting in the European Parliament. *American Journal of Political Science* 46 (3): 688–98.

Hix, Simon. 2004. *The Political System of the European Union*. 2nd ed. London: Palgrave.

Houska, Joseph J. 1985. *Influencing Mass Political Behavior: Elites and Political Subcultures in the Netherlands and Austria*. Berkeley: Institute of International Studies, University of California, Berkeley.

Huber, Evelyne, and John D. Stephens. 2001. *Development and Crisis of the Welfare State: Parties and Policies in Global Markets*. Chicago: University of Chicago Press.

Huntington, Samuel P. 1991. *The Third Wave: Democratization in the Late Twentieth Century*. Norman: University of Oklahoma Press.

Jones, Phil J., and Anders Moberg. 2003. Hemispheric and large-scale surface air temperature variations: an extensive revision and an update to 2001. *Journal of Climate* 16: 206–23.

Kassim, Hussein. 2003. The European administration: between Europeanization and administration. In *Governing Europe*, edited by Jack Hayward and Anand Menon. Oxford: Oxford University Press, 139–61.

Katz, Richard S. 1986. Party government: a rationalistic conception. In *Visions and Realities of Party Government*, edited by Francis G. Castles and Rudolf Windenmann. Florence, Berlin: EUI, de Gruyter, 31–71.

Katz, Richard S. 1987. Party government and its alternatives. In *Party Government: European and American Experience*, edited by Richard S. Katz. Florence, Berlin: EUI, de Gruyter, 1–26.

Katz, Richard S., and Peter Mair. 1992. *Party Organizations: A Data Handbook on Party Organizations in Western Democracies, 1960–90.* London: SAGE Publications.

Katz, Richard S., and Peter Mair. 1995. Changing models of party organization and party democracy: the emergence of the cartel party. *Party Politics* 1 (1): 5–28.

Katz, Richard S. 2001. Models of democracy: elite attitudes and the democratic deficit in the European Union. *European Union Politics* 2 (1): 53–80.

Katz, Richard S., and Peter Mair. 2002. The ascendency of party in public office: party organizational change in twentieth-century democracies. In *Political Parties: Old Concepts and New Challenges*, edited by Richard Gunther, José R. Montero and Juan J. Linz. Oxford: Oxford University Press, 113–35.

Katz, Richard S., and Peter Mair. 2008. MPs and parliamentary parties in the age of the cartel party. European Consortium for Political Research (ECPR) Joint Sessions, Rennes.

Katz, Richard S., and Peter Mair. 2009. The cartel party thesis: a restatement. *Perspectives on Politics* 7 (4): 753–66.

Keman, Hans. 2002. Policy-making capacities of European party government. In *Political Parties in the New Europe*, edited by K.R. Luther and Ferdinand Müller-Rommel. Oxford: Oxford University Press: 207–45.

Kelemen, R. Daniel. 2002. The politics of 'Eurocratic' structure and the new European agencies. *West European Politics* 25 (4): 93–118.

King, Anthony. 1969. Political parties in Western democracies: some sceptical reflections. *Polity* 2 (2): 111–141.

Kirchheimer, Otto. 1957. The waning of opposition in parliamentary regimes. *Social Research* 24 (2): 127–56.

Kirchheimer, Otto. 1966. The transformation of the Western European party systems. In *Political Parties and Political Development*, edited by Joseph LaPalombara and Myron Weiner. Princeton: Princeton University Press, 177–200.

Kirkpatrick, Evron M. 1971. Towards a more responsible two-party system: political science, policy science, or pseudo-science? *The American Political Science Review* 65 (4): 965–90.

Knapp, Andrew. 2004. Ephemeral victories? France's governing parties, the ecologists and the far left. In *Political Parties and Electoral Change*, edited by Peter Mair, Wolfgang C. Muller and Fritz Plasser. London: Sage, 49–85.

Knutsen, Oddbjørn. 2006. *Class Voting in Western Europe: A Comparative Longitudinal Study*. New York: Lexington Books.

Knutsen, Oddbjørn. 2007. The decline of social class? In *The Oxford Handbook of Political Behaviour* edited by Russell J. Dalton and Hans-Dieter Klingemann. Oxford University Press, 457–80.

Kohler-Koch, Beate. 2000. Framing: the bottleneck of constructing legitimate institutions. *Journal of European Public Policy* 7 (4): 513–31.

Kohler-Koch, Beate. 2005. European government and system integration. *European Governance Papers (EURGOV)* No. C-05-01. http://www.connex-network.org/eurogov/pdf/egp-connex-C-05-01.pdf

Krouwel, André. 1999. The catch-all party in Western Europe 1945–1990: a study of arrested development. Amsterdam: Vrije Universiteit (PhD).

Lafontaine, Oskar. 2000. *The Heart Beats on the Left*. Cambridge: Polity.

Lahr, John, ed. 2001. *The Diaries of Kenneth Tynan*. London: Bloomsbury.

LaPalombara, Joseph, and Myron Weiner, eds. 1966. *Political Parties and Political Development*. Studies in Political Development. Princeton: Princeton University Press.

Laver, Michael J., and Kenneth A. Shepsle. 1991. Divided government: America is not 'exceptional'. *Governance* 4 (3): 250–69.

Laver, Michael J., and Kenneth A. Shepsle. 1994. Cabinet ministers and government formation in parliamentary democracies. In *Cabinet Ministers and Parliamentary Government*, edited by Michael J. Laver and Kenneth A. Shepsle. Cambridge: Cambridge University Press, 3–12.

Lijphart, Arendt. 1968. *The Politics of Accommodation: Pluralism and Democracy in the Netherlands*. Berkeley: University of California Press.

Lijphart, Arend. 1977. *Democracy in Plural Societies: a Comparative Exploration.* New Haven: Yale University Press.

Lijphart, Arend. 1984. *Democracies: Patterns of Majoritarian and Consensus Government in Twenty-one Countries.* New Haven: Yale University Press.

Lindvall, Johannes, and Bo Rothstein. 2006. Sweden: the fall of the strong state. *Scandinavian Political Studies* 29 (1): 47–63.

Linz, Juan J. 1997. Some thoughts on the victory and future of democracy. In *Democracy's Victory and Crisis: Nobel Symposium No. 93*, edited by Alex Hadenius. Cambridge: Cambridge University Press, 404–26.

Linz, Juan J., and Alfred Stepan. 1996. *Problems of Democratic Transition and Consolidation: Southern Europe, South America, and Post-Communist Europe.* Baltimore: Johns Hopkins University Press.

Lipset, Seymour Martin, and Stein Rokkan. 1967. Cleavage structures, party systems and voter alignments: an introduction. In *Party Systems and Voter Alignments*, edited by Seymour Martin Lipset and Stein Rokkan. New York: Free Press, 1–64.

McAllister, Ian. 2002. Political parties in Australia: party stability in a utilitarian society. In *Political Parties at the Millennium: Adaptation and Decline in Democratic Societies*, edited by Paul Webb, David Farrell and Ian Holliday. Oxford: Oxford University Press, 379–408.

Mair, Peter. 1995. Political parties, popular legitimacy and public privilege. *West European Politics* 18 (3): 40–57.

Mair, Peter. 1996. Comparative politics: an overview. In *A New Handbook of Political Science*, edited by Robert Goodin and Hans-Dieter Klingemann. Oxford: Oxford University Press.

Mair, Peter. 1998. Representation and participation in the changing world of party politics. *European Review* 6 (2): 161–74.

Mair, Peter. 2000. The limited impact of Europe on national party systems. *West European Politics* 23 (4): 27–51.

Mair, Peter, and Ingrid van Biezen. 2001. Party membership in twenty European democracies, 1980–2000. *Party Politics* 7 (1): 5–21.

Mair, Peter. 2002. In the aggregate: mass electoral behaviour in Western Europe, 1950–2000. In *Comparative Democratic Politics*, edited by Hans Keman. London: Sage, 122–40.

Mair, Peter. 2004. The Europeanization dimension. *Journal of European Public Policy* 11 (2): 337–48.

Mair, Peter. 2005. Democracy beyond parties. (April 1, 2005). Center for the Study of Democracy. Paper 05-06. http://repositories.cdlib.org/csd/05-06

Mair, Peter. 2007a. Political opposition and the European Union. *Government and Opposition* 42 (1): 1–17.

Mair, Peter. 2007b. Left-right orientations. In *The Oxford Handbook of Political Behaviour*, edited by Russell J. Dalton and Hans-Dieter Klingemann. Oxford: Oxford University Press, 206–22.

Mair, Peter. 2008. Democracies. In *Comparative Politics*, edited by Daniele Caramani. Oxford: Oxford University Press, 108–32.

Mair, Peter. 2011. Smaghi *vs.* the parties: representative government and institutional constraints. Conference on Democracy in Straitjackets: Politics in an Age of Permanent Austerity, Munich.

Majone, Giandomenico. 1994. The rise of the regulatory state in Europe. *West European Politics* 17 (3): 77–101.

Majone, Giandomenico. 1996a. *Regulating Europe*. London: Routledge.

Majone, Giandomenico. 1996b. *Temporal Consistency and Policy Credibility: Why Democracies Need Non-majoritarian Institutions*. Robert Schuman Centre Working Paper 96/57. Florence: European University Institute.

Majone, Giandomenico. 2003. The politics of regulation and European regulatory institutions. In *Governing Europe*, edited by Jack Hayward and Anand Menon. Oxford: Oxford University Press. 297–312.

Manin, Bernard. 1997. *The Principles of Representative Government*. Cambridge: Cambridge University Press.

Mény, Yves, and Yves Surel, eds. 2002. *Democracies and the Populist Challenge*. Basingstoke: Palgrave.

Milward, Alan. 1992. *The European Rescue of the Nation State*. London: Routledge.

Minkenberg, Michael. 2001. The radical right in public office: agenda-setting and policy effects. *West European Politics* 24 (4): 1–21.

Moravcsik, Andrew. 1998. *The Choice for Europe*. Ithaca, NY: Cornell University Press.

Moravcsik, Andrew. 2002. In defence of the 'democratic deficit': reassessing legitimacy in the European Union. *Journal of Common Market Studies* 40 (4): 603–24.

Mudde, Cas. 2007. *Populist Radical Right Parties in Europe*. Cambridge: Cambridge University Press.

Mudde, Cas. 2008. *The Populist Radical Right: a Pathological Normalcy. Willy Brandt Series of Working Papers in International Migration and Ethnic Relations* 3 (7): 1–24.

Müller, Wolfgang C. 1994. Models of government and the Austrian cabinet. In *Cabinet Ministers and Parliamentary Government*, edited by Michael J. Laver and Kenneth A. Shepsle. Cambridge: Cambridge University Press, 15–34.

Neumann, Sigmund. 1956. *Modern Political Parties*. Chicago: University of Chicago Press.

Neunreither, Karlheinz. 2000. Political representation in the European Union: a common whole, various wholes, or just a hole? In *European Integration After Amsterdam*, edited by Karlheinz Neunreither and Antje Wiener. Oxford: Oxford University Press, 129–50.

Neyer, Jürgen. 2000. Justifying comitology: the promise of deliberation. In *European Integration After Amsterdam*, edited by Karlheinz Neunreither and Antje Wiener. Oxford: Oxford University Press, 112–28.

Norris, Pippa. 2002. *Democratic Phoenix: Reinventing Political Activism*. Cambridge: Cambridge University Press.

O'Brien, Flann. 1967. *The Third Policeman*. London: McGibbon and Kee.

Paterson, Thomas E. 2002. *The Vanishing Voter: Public Involvement in an Age of Uncertainty*. New York: Knopf.

Pedersen, Mogens N. 1979. The dynamics of European party systems: changing patterns of electoral volatility. *European Journal of Political Research* 7 (1): 1–26.

Peters, B. Guy. 2002. *Governance: a Garbage Can Perspective*. Political Science Series, Institute for Advanced Studies. Vienna, December.

Peters, B. Guy. 2003. Dismantling and rebuilding the Weberian state. In *Governing Europe*, edited by Jack Hayward and Anand Menon. Oxford: Oxford University Press, 113–27.

Pettit, Philip. 1998. Republican theory and political trust. In *Trust and Governance*, edited by Valerie Braithwaite and Margaret Levi. New York: Russell Sage Foundation, 295–314.

Pettit, Philip. 2001. Deliberative democracy and the case for depoliticizing government. *University of NSW Law Journal 58*.

Pijpers, Alfred. 1999. *De mythe van het democratisch tekort Een discussiebijdrage over de Europese politiek*. The Hague: Clingendael Institute.

Pizzorno, Alessandro. 1981. Interests and parties in pluralism. In *Organized Interests in Western Europe: Pluralism, Corporatism, and the Transformation of Politics*, edited by Suzanne Berger. Cambridge: Cambridge University Press, 249–84.

Poguntke Thomas. 2000. *Parteienorganisatie im Wandel: Gesellschaftliche Verankerung und organisatorische Anpassung im europäischen Vergleich*. Weisbaden: Westdeutscher Verlag.

Poguntke, Thomas. 2005. Parteien ohne (an)bindung: verkümmern die organisatorsichen wurzeln der parteien? In *Zwischen Anarchie und Strategie. Der Erfolg von Parteiorganisationen*, edited by Josef Schmid and Udo Zolleis. Wiesbaden: Verlag für Sozialwissenschaften, 43–62.

Poguntke, Thomas, and Paul D. Webb. 2005. *The Presidentialization of Politics: a Comparative Study of Modern Democracies*.

Przeworski, Adam, and Henry Teune. 1970. *The Logic of Comparative Social Inquiry*. New York: Wiley.

Ranney, Austin. 1978. Introduction. In *Euro-communism: The Italian Case*, edited by Austin Ranney and Giovanni Sartoti. Washington, DC: American Enterprise Institute, 1–5.

Rawnsley, Andrew. 2000. *Servants of the People: The Inside Story of New Labour*. London: Penguin.

Rose, Richard. 1969. The variability of party government: a theoretical and empirical critique. *Political Studies* 17 (4): 413–45.

Rose, Richard. 1974. *The Problem of Party Government*. New York: Free Press.

Rose, Richard. 1980. *Do Parties Make a Difference?* New York: Macmillan.

Rose, Richard, and Harve Mossawir. 1967. Voting and elections: a functional analysis. *Political Studies* 15 (2): 173–201.

Roth, Guenther. 1963. *The Social Democrats in Imperial Germany: A Study in Working-Class Isolation and National Integration*. Somerville: Bedminster Press.

Ruggie, John Gerard. 1982. International regimes, transactions, and change: embedded liberalism in the postwar economic order. *International Organization* 36 (2): 379–415.

Ruggie John G. 1997. Globalization and the embedded liberalism compromise: the end of an era? MPIfG Working Paper, 97/1.

Sandholz, Wayne, and Alec Stone Sweet, eds. 1998. *European Integration and Supranational Governance*. Oxford: Oxford University Press.

Sani, Giacomo, and Giovanni Sartori. 1983. Polarization, fragmentation and competition in western democracies. In *West European Party Systems:Continuity and Change*, edited by Hans Daalder and Peter Mair. Beverley Hills: Sage, 307–40.

Sartori, Giovanni. 1970. Concept misformation in comparative politics. *American Political Science Review* 64 (4): 1033–53.

Sartori, Giovanni. 1976. *Parties and Party Systems: A Framework for Analysis*. Cambridge: Cambridge University Press.

Sartori, Giovanni. 2002. *Homo Videns*. Rome: Economia Laterza.

Sartre, Jean-Paul. 1963. *The Problem of Method*. London: Methuen.

Sauger, Nicolas. 2007. The French presidential and legislative elections of 2007. *West European Politics* 30 (5): 1166–75.

Scarrow, Susan E. 2000. Parties without members? party organization in a changing electoral environment. In *Parties Without Partisans: Political Change in Advanced Industrial Democracies*, edited by Russell J. Dalton and Martin P. Wattenberg. Oxford: Oxford University Press, 79–101.

Scharpf, Fritz. 1999. *Governing in Europe: Effective and Democratic?* Oxford: Oxford University Press.

Scharpf, Fritz W. 2000. Economic changes, vulnerabilities and institutional capabilities. In *Welfare and Work in the Open Economy, Vol. 1: From Vulnerability to Competitiveness*, edited by Fritz W. Scharpf and Vivien A. Schmidt. Oxford: Oxford University Press, 21–124.

Schattschneider, Elmer E. 1942. *Party Government*. New York: Holt, Rinehart and Winston.

Schattschneider, Elmer E. 1945. Party government and employment policy. *The American Political Science Review* 39 (6): 1147–57.

Schattschneider, Elmer E. 1960. *The Semi-sovereign People. A Realist's View of Democracy in America*. New York: Wadsworth.

Schmidt, Manfred G. 1996. When parties matter: a review of the possibilities and limits of partisan influence on public policy. *European Journal of Political Research* 30 (2): 155–83.

Schmitter, Phillipe C. 2001. Parties are not what they once were. In *Political Parties and Democracy*, edited by Larry Diamond and Richard Gunther. Baltimore: The Johns Hopkins University Press, 67–89.

Schumpeter, Joseph A. 1947. *Capitalism, Socialism, and Democracy*. 2nd edition. New York: Harper and Brothers.

Shaw, Jo. 2000. Constitutional settlements and the citizen after the Treaty of Amsterdam. In *European Integration After Amsterdam*, edited by Karlheinz Neunreither and Antje Wiener. Oxford: Oxford University Press.

Shepsle, Kenneth A. 1995. Studying institutions: some lessons from the rational choice approach. In *Political Science in*

History, edited by James Farr, John S. Dryzek and Stephen T. Leonard. Cambridge: Cambridge University Press.

Smith, Gordon. 1986. The futures of party government: a framework for analysis. In *Visions and Realities of Party Government*, edited by Francis G. Castles and Rudolf Wildenmann. Florence, Berlin: EUI, de Gruyter, 31–71.

Smith, Gordon. 1989. Core persistence: change and the 'people's party'. *West European Politics* 12 (4): 157–68.

Statera, Giovanni. 1986. *La Politica Spettacolo*, Milan: Mondadori.

Stone Sweet, Alec, and Mark Thatcher. 2002. Theory and practice of delegation to non-majoritarian institutions. *West European Politics* 25 (1): 1–22.

Strøm, Kaare, Wolfgang C. Muller and Torbjörn Bergman, eds. 2003. Challenges to parliamentary democracy. In *Delegation and Accountability in Parliamentary Democracies*, edited by Kaare Strøm, Wolfgang C. Muller and Torbjørn Bergman. Oxford: Oxford University Press, 707–50.

Strøm, Kaare, Wolfgang C. Müller and Torbjörn Bergman, eds. 2003. *Delegation and Accountability in Parliamentary Democracies*. Oxford: Oxford University Press.

Thaa, Winfried. 2001. 'Lean citizenship': the fading away of the political in transnational democracy. *European Journal of International Relations* 7 (4): 503–23.

Thatcher, Mark, and Alec Stone Sweet, eds. 2003. *The Politics of Delegation*. London: Cass.

Thomassen, Jacques. 1994. Empirical research into political representation: failing democracy or failing models? In *Elections at Home and Abroad: Essays in Honor of Warren Miller*, edited by M. Kent Jennings and Thomas E. Mann. Ann Arbor: Michigan University Press, 237–65.

Thomassen, Jacques, and Hermann Schmitt. 1999. In conclusion: political representation and legitimacy in the European Union. In *Political Representation and Legitimacy in the European Union*, edited by Hermann Schmitt and Jacques Thomassen. Oxford: Oxford University Press, 255–73.

Tocqueville, Alexis de. 1966. *The Ancien Regime and the French Revolution*, trans. Stuart Gilbert. Glasgow: Collins.

Tocqueville, Alexis de. 1966. *Democracy in America*. New York: Harper & Row.

Valen, Henry. 1976. National conflict structures and foreign politics: the impact of the EEC issue on perceived cleavages in Norwegian politics. *European Journal of Political Research* 4 (1): 47–82.

Van Biezen, Ingrid. 2003. *Financing Political Parties and Election Campaigns: Guidelines*. Strasbourg: Council of Europe Publishing.

Van Biezen, Ingrid, Peter Mair and Thomas Poguntke. 2012. Going, going ... gone? The decline of party membership in contemporary Europe. *European Journal of Political Research* 51 (1): 24–56.

Van Deth, Jan W. 2000. Interesting but irrelevant: social capital and the saliency of politics in Western Europe. *European Journal of Political Research* 37 (2): 115–47.

Van Spanje, Joos, and Wouter van der Brug. 2007. The Party as pariah – ostracism of anti-immigration parties and its effect on their ideological positions. *West European Politics* 30 (5): 1022–40.

Vowles, Jack. 2002. Parties in society in New Zealand. In *Political Parties in Advanced Industrial Democracies*, edited by Paul Webb, David Farrell and Ian Holliday. Oxford: Oxford University Press, 409–37.

Weale, Albert. 1997. Democratic theory and the constitutional politics of the European Union. *Journal of European Public Policy* 4 (4): 665–69.

Webb, Paul, David Farrell and Ian Holliday, eds. 2002. *Political Parties in Advanced Industrial Democracies*. Oxford: Oxford University Press.

Widfeldt, Anders. 1995. Party membership and party representativeness. In *Citizens and the States*, edited by Hans-Dieter Klingemann and Dieter Fuchs. Oxford: Oxford University Press, 134–83.

Wildenmann, Rudolf. 1986. The problematic of party government. In *Visions and Realities of Party Government*, edited by Francis G. Castles and Rudolf Wildenmann. Florence, Berlin: EUI, de Gruyter, 1–30.

Zakaria, Fareed. 1997. The rise of illiberal democracy. *Foreign Affairs* 76 (6): 22–43.

Zakaria, Fareed. 2003. *The Future of Freedom: Illiberal Democracy at Home and Abroad*. New York: Norton.

INDEX

Page numbers in *italics* refer to
tables

Almond, Gabriel A. 89n, 121,
122, 123, 124
American Political Science
Association 60
Andeweg, Rudy 22, 94, 128
Andreotti, Giulio 47, 48
Association of South-East
Asian Nations 19
Australia 36, 40n
Austria 19, 24, 25, 26, 28, 32,
33, 35, 38, 40, 41, 41, 110,
112–13
Freedom Party 46

Bagehot, Walter 18n
Bale, Tim 66
Barroso, José Manuel 104
Bartolini, Stefano xiii, 30, 33,
79, 88, 106n, 132
Beck, Ulrich 4, 18

Belgium 24, 25, 27, 28, 32, 33,
35, 36, 38, 41, 112–13,
121
Bellamy, Richard 111, 120,
128
Bennett, W. Lance 18n, 34n
Berger, Suzanne 72–73
Bergman, Torbjörn 76
Bertram, Christopher 133n
Best, Robin E. 56
Beyers, Jan 125, 136, 139n
Beyme, Klaus von 95n
Blair, Tony 3–4, 48, 67, 93n
Blinder, Alan S. 5
Blocher, Christoph 19
Blondel, Jean 65n, 81
Blyth, Mark 129
Boix, Carles 54
Börzel, Tanja 139n
Bossi, Umberto 19
Bretton Woods system 55
Brittan, Samuel 133
Brown, Gordon 67, 94

Buller, Jim 4
Burnham, Peter 51
Buttiglione, Rocco 104

Cameron, David 76
Canada 36, 40n
Caporaso, James 120n
Cardoso, Fernando Henrique 48
Carter, Jimmy 47
Carty, R.K. 40n, 118n
Castles, Francis G. 53, 81
Catalonia 119n
Caul, Miki 54
China 101
Christiansen, Thomas 136–37, 137n
Chua, Amy 11, 15
Clinton, Bill 48
Cold War xi, 13, 49, 101
Collier, David 7
Cotta, Maurizio 65n, 81, 89
Cowles, Maria Green, et al. 105
Cox, Gary W. 96
Curtin, Deirdre 134

Daalder, Hans 60
Dahl, Robert 10, 88, 133, 138, 140–42
D'Alema, Massimo 48–49
Dalton, Russell J. 14–15, 35–36, 35, 39, 58
Dalton, Russell J., et al. 30
Denmark 19, 25, 27, 28, 31, 32, 33, 35, 36, 37, 38, 41, 112–13
    June Movement 109n, 112n
    People's Movement Against the EU 109n, 112n
    People's Party 46
DeWinter, Lieven 19, 96n

Diamond, Larry 10, 102
Doorenspleet, Renske 100
Downs, William M. 46n

Easton, David 121
van der Eijk, Cees 110–11
Eisenstadt, S.N. 10n
Elff, Martin 56
Eriksen, Erik Oddvar 127, 135, 137
European Central Bank 59, 115–16
European Commission 7, 104, 117, 127, 134
    President 48
European Council 104
European Economic Community xiv
European Free Trade Association 59
European Parliament 104–5, 107–8, 109–10, 110n, 117–18, 127, 136–37
European Union xv, 7, 9, 19, 59, 76, 91, 99–112, 112–13, 115–42
    Council of Ministers 104, 134
    Growth and Stability Pact 59
Europol 115–16
Everson, Michelle 11–12, 103

Falconer, Charles (Lord) 4
Featherstone, Kevin 105
Finer, S.E. 49–50, 122
Finland 25, 26, 28, 32, 33, 35, 38, 41, 112–13
    True Finns 112n
Flanders 19
Flinders, Matthew 4, 117, 134n

Fortuyn, Pim 20n
Fossum, John Erik 127, 135, 137
France 19, 24, 25–26, 26, 28, 28, 31, 32, 33, 35, 38, 41, 41, 51, 59, 80, 110, 112–13, 123–24
Franklin, Mark N. 22–23, 24, 30, 57, 110–11
Freedom House 100n
Freire, Paulo 57

Gallagher, Michael xiii
Garrett, Geoffrey 53–54
Germany 25, 28, 31, 32, 33, 36, 41, 41, 112–13
  Christian Democrats 52
  Green Party 52
  Social Democratic Party (SDP) 52, 67
  West 38
Germany, imperial 80
Giddens, Anthony 43, 93
Goetz, Klaus H. 105
Grabbe, Heather 115
Gray, Mark 54
Greece 26, 28, 41, 66, 112–13
Gustavsson, Sverker 120

Hadenius, Axel 12, 100
Hailsham (Quintin Hogg, Lord Hailsham) 50
Hardin, Russell 71–72
Heinisch, Reinhard 46n
Héritier, Adrienne 135
Hix, Simon 105, 122n
Houska, Joseph J. 79
Huber, Evelyne 54
Huntington, Samuel P. 100

Iceland 28, 32, 33, 35, 38

International Monetary Fund 19
IRA (Irish Republican Army) 46
Ireland xiv–xv, 26, 28, 32, 33, 35, 41, 79, 112–13
  Fianna Fáil 52, 80
  Fine Gael 52
  Labour Party 52
  Sinn Féin 46, 112n
Italy xiv, 19, 28, 32, 33, 35, 38, 41, 41, 112–13, 119n
  Christian Democrat (DC) 47
  Italian Communist Party (PCI) 46–48
  Italian Social Movement (MSI) 47
  National Alliance 46
  Party of the Democratic Left (DS) 48–49

Jenkins, Roy 114n
Jones, Phil 27
Jospin, Lionel 48

Kassim, Hussein 122n
Katz, Richard S. xv, 18, 38, 61–63, 64, 65n, 70, 83, 85, 89, 129, 136n, 140n
Katz, Richard S. et al. 40
Keman, Hans 53, 56
Kerremans, Bert 125, 136
King, Anthony 89n
Kirchheimer, Otto 68, 82, 85n
Kirkpatrick, Evron M. 60
Kissinger, Henry 47–48, 49
Klein, Joe 111n, 133n
Knutsen, Oddbjørn 56–57
Kohler-Koch, Beate 15, 127n
Krouwel, André 95

Lafontaine, Oskar 67, 131
Lahr, John 114n
Lamy, Pascal 111n
LaPalombara, Joseph 91
Laver, Michael J. xiii, 52n, 63n
Le Pen, Marine 19
Levitsky, Steven 7
Lijphart, Arendt 6n, 79, 101–2, 121
Lindvall, Johannes 69–70
Linz, Juan J. 12, 100–101, 102
Lipset, Seymour Martin 78, 106–7
Luther, Kurt Richard 96n
Luxembourg 28, *28*, 32, *33*, *35*, *112–13*

McAllister, Ian 40n
McCubbins, Mathew Daniel 96
McGahern, John xiv–xv
Majone, Giandomenico 5–6, 11–12, 69, 124, 133, 136
Malta 66
Manin, Bernard 43–44, 83n
Mény, Yves 10n
Milward, Alan 131
Minkenberg, Michael 46n
Moberg, Anders 27
Moravcsik, Andrew 126, 136n
Mossawir, Harve 78
Mudde, Cas 19, 45
Müller-Rommel, Ferdinand 96n
Müller, Wolfgang C. 63n, 76

Neo-liberalism 53
Netherlands xiv, 19, 24, *25*, *28*, 31, 32, *33*, *35*, 38, 41, *41*, 51–52, 79, 110, *112–13*

Labour Party 52
Liberal Party 52
Pim Fortuyn List 46
Neumann, Sigmund 79, 93
Neunreither, Karlheinz 120
New Public Management 12
New Zealand 40n
Neyer, Jurgen 136
Norris, Pippa 22, 24, 39
Northern Ireland 121
Bloody Sunday xiv
Sinn Féin 46
Norway 19, 24, *25*, 26, *28*, 31, 32, *33*, *35*, 38, 41, *41*, 42, *42*, 119n

O'Brien, Flann 139n

Paterson, Thomas E. 29n
Pedersen, Mogens 30–31
Peters, B. Guy 4, 12
Pettit, Philip 9, 15, 103
Pijpers, Alfred 118n, 137n
Pizzorno, Alessandro 91
Poguntke, Thomas 68, 85n, 92n
Portugal 26, 28, *41*, 66, *112–13*
Prodi, Romano 48
Przeworski, Adam 123

Radelli, Claudio M. 105
Rawnsley, Andrew 67n
Reagan, Ronald 53
Risse, Thomas 139n
Rokkan, Stein 78, 106–7
Rome, Treaty of 126
Rose, Richard 52, 61, 62, 63, 64, 69, 70, 78
Rothstein, Bo 69–70
Ruggie, John Gerard 13, 55, 72

Ryanair 116

Sandholz, Wayne 126
Sani, Giacomo 70
Sartori, Giovanni 44, 70, 122,
    141n
Sartre, Jean-Paul 124n
Sauger, Nicolas 59
Scarrow, Susan E. 39
Scharpf, Fritz 55, 72, 134, 136
Schattschneider, E.E. 1–2,
    13–16, 60
Schmidt, Manfred G. 53,
    55–56
Schmitter, Philippe 91n
Schmitt, Hermann 108, 125n,
    138
Schröder, Gerhard 48, 67
Schumpeter, Joseph A. 102,
    133
Schwarzenegger, Arnold 95
Scotland xiii–xiv
Shaw, Jo 9, 120
Shepsle, Kenneth A. 52n, 63n,
    101
Smith, Gordon 65n, 140n
Soviet Union 46, 101
Spain 26, 28, 41, 66, 112–13
Statera, Giovanni 44n
Stepan, Alfred 12, 101
Stephens, John 54
Stone Sweet, Alec 12, 69, 116,
    126
Strache, Heinz-Christian 19
Strøm, Kaare, 116
Strøm, Karl 76
Surel, Yves 10n
Sweden 25, 27, 28, 32, 33,
    35, 36, 38, 41, 41, 69–70,
    112–13
Switzerland 19, 25, 26, 28, 32,
    33, 41, 121

Teune, Henry 123
Thaa, Winfried 109, 132
Thatcher, Margaret 49–50, 53
Thatcher, Mark 12, 69, 116
Third Way 48, 50–51, 93
Thomassen, Jacques 63–64,
    70–71, 108, 125n, 138
Tocqueville, Alexis de 3, 130
Toynbee, Polly 93n
Trondal, Jade 139n
Turkey 111
Tynan, Ken 114n

United Kingdom 25, 26, 28,
    33, 35, 38, 41, 41, 76, 95,
    100, 110, 112–13
    Conservative Party 49–50
    Labour Party 49, 50, 67,
        80, 94
    New Labour 50–51
    Thatcher governments
        49–50
    United Kingdom
        Independence Party
        112n
United States of America xv,
    5, 24, 36, 47–48, 60, 79,
    96, 100
    California 95
    Federal Reserve 5
    State Department 47, 49

Valen, Henry 119n
Van Biezen, Ingrid 37, 39, 40,
    41, 86n
Van der Brug, Wouter 46n
Van Deth, Jan W. 3
Van Spanje, Joos 46n
Vowles, Jack 40n

Warleigh, Alex 111, 120,
    128

Wattenberg, Martin P. 14–15,
    35–36
Weale, Albert 127–28
Webb, Paul 68
Weiner, Myron 91
West Germany 38
White, Michael 93n, 94n
Widfeldt, Anders 38

Wildenmann, Rudolf 81
Wilders, Geert 19
World Bank 7
World Trade Organization 19

Zakaria, Fareed 9, 10–11, 15,
    102, 103, 132–33